Finding Francis

By

Cristina T. Lopez

ISBN: 1-4107-2547-2 (e-book)
ISBN: 1-4107-2546-4 (Paperback)

This book is printed on acid free paper.

1stBooks - rev. 05/03/03

Table of Contents

Introduction

Perhaps now is a good time for me, in the distinguished tradition of Saint Augustine, to confess: I am extremely ignorant of geography. Somehow, transferring between grade schools midway through my elementary career, I missed the essential geography lesson that delineates between the Dakotas, characterizes the Carolinas, and separates Iowa from Ohio. It is only recently that I've stared at maps and oriented myself to my state, country and the globe. While the idea of identifying Asian borders and small tropical islands on a map still terrifies me, I'm trying to overcome that fear and learn what I have inadvertently missed.

At this point in time, you might be asking: "Why? What is the purpose of this statement?" The statement comes from a need in me to reveal my faults, my imperfections. It seems a little thing, but huge when you consider what I'm up against: the notion of author omniscience. This idea of the writer as all-knowing is frightening to someone taking up her pen for the first time. While others may scoff and bravely take on the challenge of knowing more, of guiding, I cannot.

I don't want you to come to these pages seeking out answers. I want you to approach these pages and walk away with more questions. Whether difficult or simple, improper or relevant, the question is an attempt to satisfy the burning curiosity within. And isn't that the substance of every great search?

CTL

20 June 1997

Second Introduction

Wow, did that suck or what? I just re-read that introduction I wrote three years ago and I hate it. What was I thinking? How pretentious could I be?

I guess what I was trying to get at was that I don't know anything. I'm not writing this to teach you something because you probably know a hell of a lot more than I do. I'm not trying to shove any religious or political beliefs down your throat. I don't have a hidden agenda. Well, I do, but if you're reading this book, I've already accomplished it.

I just want to tell you a story. It is definitely my own story but I think that you may find you have felt some of the same emotions that I experienced while searching for Francis. Maybe you have a Francis in your own life: a long lost friend, soul mate or acquaintance you wonder about; someone you have looked for or someone you have not actually sought out.

My goal is to share my story and hopefully make you understand why it doesn't matter what you are looking for. Sometimes just looking is the most important part. And the things you find may surprise you.

I didn't mean for this to become a love story but in so many ways it is: my love of writing, romantic love and, of course, the love of endlessly talking about myself. Sorry about the last part but I'm just as pretentious as that first introduction made me out to be and it's my book, so suck it up.

I'd like to dedicate this book to everyone - every single person I have known or met. I know that statement will piss off my parents but, as I hope you'll see from this story, every person we encounter in our lives has an effect on us and vice versa. They may not know it, you may not know it, but it's true.

So to that lady in front of me at Keyfood, the guy who picked his nose at the red light on Queens Boulevard, the kid who almost ran me down this morning walking her Doberman, I dedicate this book to you. You've made me who I am, some more than others of course, but everyone touches us. Often we wish they didn't, like that gross guy on the subway, but that you cannot help. All I can suggest is that you go with it and relish it a bit.

Our personal stories are compilations of contact and impact. This is mine. I hope you find it interesting.

CTL

30 October 2000

I. The Beginning

Cristina T. Lopez

About Six

Twenty years ago I was six years old. I cared nothing about being six. I enjoyed my childhood and I was happy but all I truly wanted in life was to be seven.

For me, seven was grand. Seven was special. Seven was my lucky number. On the number puzzle I got for my sixth birthday, the seven was pink with bunnies. Six had bugs all over it. Seven was going to be my First Holy Communion, learning script and having Mrs. Carlos as a teacher.

Mrs. Carlos was wonderful before I ever stepped foot in her classroom. She had a warm smile, was very pretty and often wore pink. Best of all, her students were always happy. They all seemed special to her. She was the kind of woman who would talk to you and make you feel like you were the only girl in the world. She was the kind of teacher who would take you to McDonald's™ if you forgot your lunch or spend an afternoon leading the class in their favorite songs.

Yes, seven was the pinnacle. Everything before it was just passing time. At six, it would take something significant to grab my attention from seven. It would take something unusual for me to stop and take notice.

Enter Francis.

Francis sat behind me in the only first grade class at All Saints School. Our teacher was Mrs. Sinow and, let me tell you, she was no Mrs. Carlos. She was very stern and serious, not mean or cruel, but a teacher who never sparked smiles from her students. Almost everything about Mrs. Sinow was boring and uninteresting. Everything except one thing: rumor had it that she wore a wig.

To adults, a wig may have been nothing, but to a group of six-year-olds this was like finding out she was a robot. Her every move was scrutinized and noted for evidence of wig-wearing: how she confiscated the rubber bands that the boys flung across the room; how she always put the rubber bands on her wrists; how she was seen several times a day tucking her fingers beneath her bowl-cut hair. What was she tucking? Was she straightening her hairpiece? Were her fingers securing the rubber bands that she had stolen from the little boys? She smelled of hairspray. It must've been a wig - or so it seemed to our outrageous and overactive imaginations.

It was our imaginations, our small conspiracies that drew us closer together at such a young age. But, although clusters of friends were beginning to develop, most social activity was still dictated by school functions and parental supervised play dates. Most parents wanted their children to have many friends, or at least appear to, so most birthday parties had guest lists of the entire class, sometimes cousins and neighbors. Francis Laboure's family was no exception.

As far as I can remember, it was the end of school, probably June. I was invited to Francis' birthday party, which was to be held on a Saturday afternoon. The exact date is fuzzy in my mind because the only information I was actually given was that I was a guest at this celebration. My mom wrote down the date, bought the gift, picked out my attire and arranged my transportation.

Francis was an average boy. In retrospect, he was cute, but in first grade I had not noticed. All the boys were small and cute, except Michael who used to eat peanut butter and jelly sandwiches and, with gooey mouth and hands, try to kiss me during recess. Francis was blond and blue-eyed, quiet and shy. When we did phonics exercises I could hear a slight lisp. It was uncertain whether it was permanent or there due to his recently missing front baby teeth.

Francis was the opposite of the loud and rambunctious boys of the class. He was calm with a hushed voice, probably stemming from embarrassment about his lisp. My memories of him are minimal, perhaps because he faded somewhat into the backdrop. I had no particularly strong feelings for him one way or the other. But apparently some others did.

It was a completely normal Saturday afternoon as I was driven to Queens Village for Francis' party. By normal I mean I don't recall any earthquakes or tornadoes pending in the area, no flashflood warnings were in effect for the Tri-State area and I believe our car was in working condition.

Francis and his mom happily greeted me at the door. As I stepped into the living room, the huge cake on display in the dining room table was visible. So was the large, white, elaborate candle apparently given at his baptism and which was to be burned every year on his birthday. There were balloons and some streamers, bowls of candy and chips. I was thrilled.

Apparently, I was uncharacteristically early since I was the only guest there when I arrived. The Laboures were definitely prepared for a big crowd with stacks of board games in the living room and a virtual obstacle course set up in the backyard with classic games like pin-the-tail-on-the donkey. At first I was very excited for the activities and, of course, the cake, but as time went by it soon became evident that I was the only person to take part. No one else ever came to Francis' party.

I vaguely remember the different family members trying to distract us with games so we wouldn't realize that no one else was coming. I overheard Francis' mother on the phone, perhaps with a friend, explaining that there were a lot of graduations this time of year. I did not understand the connection to a graduation and no one coming to the party when they said they would.

Later, I recall Francis crying and not wanting to play with me. His older sister gave me a tour of her room so he could be alone. I walked into a medium-sized bedroom with colorful butterflies dancing on the wallpaper behind posters of teen idols. I remember Scott Baio in tight jeans. I remember how cool I thought she was.

Then came the unbelieving look on my mom's face when she came to get me and saw I was still the only guest there; the banter of excuses as to why people hadn't come; and, the piles of candy I was allowed to leave with since there was no one else there to take it. I remember returning to school Monday and beginning the countdown to the end of the year: a time filled with tests, parties and good-byes. I don't remember talking about the party with anyone. I don't remember seeing Francis again after his party. The school year ended.

We often traveled during the summer or spent a lot of time at the beach so I rarely saw most of my school friends in between grades. When I returned to All Saints in September to start second grade, Francis Laboure was no longer enrolled. I don't recall asking why or talking about it with anyone else. By then I was in the glory of second grade. I was in Mrs. Carlos' class every single day of the week. We had creative writing contests and arts and crafts. I played hopscotch every day. I was about to turn seven. There was too much to look forward to and little reason to turn back.

Eventually, six was shattered into tiny pieces in my memory: broken fragments whose individual recollections were sharp but which overall dulled within months, faded in years. Francis was part of those memories. As time quickly went by, eventually seven was gone too. It vanished, like Mrs. Carlos who left to have a baby.

Then eight was gone. Then nine. Slowly my age became other ages added together. It wasn't until I passed twenty that I stopped to catch my breath. By then, all the tiny fragments of long ago had been buried deep in the rubble. But they were not gone, only waiting to be sifted, waiting to be found.

<u>The Francis Fandango</u>

It was a Saturday afternoon twenty years later at the Bronx Zoo when my boyfriend, Tom, and I, looking for the Mouse House, encountered the Butterfly Exhibit: a sealed tent creating a habitat in which the butterflies could fly freely. Spectators were encouraged not to touch the fragile butterflies, but as I walked around reading the descriptive signs and explanations, watching butterflies land in the hair of small children who ran to their parents to take photographs, I noticed the look on Tom's face. It was the same look he had when we went to see the Turtle Farm in the Cayman Islands: an expression of wonder and mischief that transforms the face of a twenty-six-year-old man into that of a nine-year-old boy as he grabs the turtle by the back legs "just to see how hard he can kick."

I could see that plotting expression on Tom's face in the butterfly tent as the beautiful creatures fluttered around our heads. I knew he wanted to grab one, "just one," to see what it would feel like, what would happen. It took every ounce of his self-control to not capture one

11

and poke it with a stick. I could see that other part of him trying to wrestle control. But he never gave in. Not even in the gift shop where most adults tend to release their inner child.

As I pondered Tom's self-control, a butterfly danced close to my periphery and I felt myself disappear for a split second. In a blink, I was surrounded by butterflies but in a different place. I remembered a bedroom and a wall covered with butterflies. I tried to place myself and realized I was remembering the bedroom of Francis' sister from so long ago. Vague recollections of Chachi in tight jeans flooded my head and I felt again my petty jealousy rise as I stood in her adolescent bedroom being just a little girl that she was trying to distract from her brother's tantrum. I remembered the desperate feeling of wanting to be older, of wanting to be something else and how it overwhelmed me. I couldn't wait for my transformation. Now, here I was, so many years later, standing in the zoo being that "someone else," living that transformation. Was I what I had envisioned myself as becoming?

I had not always wanted to be a writer but I think that identity has suited me, despite its fluctuations. Depending on the status of my current project, I could either be proud of my achievements or unwilling to even admit I write. When a project is successful, I want the world to know. When I'm blocked, I wish I were an accountant or chemical engineer, anything but a writer. During this particular time in my life, I was admitting my identity as a writer but it was a tentative achievement at best. I had a book in full swing but no idea how to resolve it.

My book was about finding my grammar school peer, Francis, and writing about the experience. People I told about the book loved the story, a heart-wrenching tale of finding someone from the past, but the inevitable question always emerged: have you found him? Have you located Francis?

My reply was always: "You'll have to read the book." But in my mind I would be saying: "AHHHHHHHHH! No, I haven't found him! Leave me alone already!"

I understood the curiosity other people had. It made sense that everyone wanted the big Francis reunion scene. The Francis Fandango. The Francis Flamenco. I mean, the book *is* called *Finding Francis*. I'm not stupid. But I had other ideas.

For example, I saw the effect the butterflies had on the zoogoers that day. They were captivating, beautiful, colorful, alive, but, at some point in time, they were ugly worms that couldn't fly and never fluttered. Most spectators would not want to check out the "Closet of Caterpillars" or the "Worm Winnebago." The Butterfly Tent was different, magical, partly because it was like looking through a window into a dancing, sparkling world of color, but also because it was like looking in the mirror and being able to see your own potential.

That day in the Bronx Zoo I realized how much I had changed, how much happier I was with myself and how I had blossomed into a different person. I wanted to talk about that, explore the transformation as part of the process of finding someone else. Wasn't all that worth mentioning in a book?

Well, perhaps not. Even though for the first time in my life I noticed that my life was full of butterflies, full of dazzling beauty and ordinary possibility, it was not enough. Even though I looked around and saw all my friends transformed into new beings, but all growing up and out of insecurities and into new bodies and minds, it was not enough. It mattered little that we all didn't become beautiful butterflies, but we were special, unique and new, something that it isn't always easy to see when you yourself are changing.

The beauty of the transformation was not the story people wanted to read. It was the discovery of Francis that had their pulses racing and minds fluttering with possibility. The reunion of two lost souls was the story that begged to be told. I had to deliver this sad, tragic hero to my readers. I had to find him again and bring him to the forefront of these pages. But I did not know how. Hence my afternoon escape to the Butterfly Tent at the Bronx Zoo.

As the zoo's massive exiting crowd absorbed us, I pondered all the families, all the faces, making their way to their cars. License plates from New York, New Jersey, Connecticut and more littered the overflowing parking lot. Any one of these people could be Francis. I did not know where to start. It all seemed so easy in a conversation, in an e-mail, but the nature of the beast is so much more complicated.

I slid into the plush seat of the old station wagon Tom and I stormed around in those days for adventures like visits to the zoo or evenings at the movies. I felt that the car had history for us. He picked me up for our first date in that car. On long drives down the Grand Central Parkway, we got to know one another. Now he knew me well, testament to those many drives as well as the interest he took in me, especially my writing.

Tom was no stranger to my plight of finding Francis. He had no choice but to accept this random obsession with another man from my past. He took me at my word that Francis was not an ex-boyfriend, that I had not seen him for twenty years. He accepted it without question but perhaps that was not hard for him as he took it as part of my being a writer. He only knew me as a writer, not the closet-hack who could never admit her artistic intentions. Perhaps that made it different, us different.

I think back to that time, the person I was before, the person I had been for so long, and try to find Tom a place in that life. It is difficult. I went through many phases of myself before I met him and it is hard to see where he might have fit in before we met. He stepped in just at the right moment when I was ready for him. I was hoping maybe the same might happen with Francis.

Well, hoping and dreading at the same time. What if Francis was as ready for me as I was for Tom? What if it wasn't just me finding him to reconnect? What if there was more to the situation and that something more was what brought me to him, something cosmic at play? This was the secret of finding Francis I never shared with Tom: the fear that maybe Francis was somehow my soul mate.

The romantic tie to Francis in my story had been suggested to me many times by others who had heard the story. I had little evidence to deny or agree so I left it untouched. But it was present. Perhaps I was vulnerable to it when I had begun to search for him. Anything was possible. I delved into finding Francis just before graduating from college, a time filled with change and uncertainty for the future. I was preparing to shed the cocoon of my college existence and enter the working world.

<u>Homecoming</u>

I remember the feeling of inevitability during those last few months of senior year of college. I sensed that things were about to change and there was nothing I could do about it. I was overly emotional and sentimental about everything. I found myself fondly reminiscing about items from my youth that I had previously found torturous: my pale ink comforter, my pink gingham pillows, the pink glass table lamp in a room wallpapered with dancing pink ballerinas. Suddenly, the Pepto Bismol-laced nightmare was quaint instead of the shame of my teenage life. Somehow my old house had become the symbol of a previous life and comforts that I was becoming reluctant to leave behind.

The Easter holiday approached and I acted as if it would be my last. I rearranged my hectic class and study schedule to make the trip home because I wanted to be in my house one last time as a student, as a youth, as a child, before it all changed. It was certainly melodramatic but the journey home was soothing. The familiar trip gave me a sense of comfort and control. The bus ride back to my old neighborhood made me feel like I had a tie to the past that could not be severed, no matter how turbulent my life seemed to be.

Fresh Meadows, Queens may sound like a place where butterflies roam and fly free, but to me it was a nest where time stood still. No matter how much I spread my wings, I always flew back home. Home was safe. I was loved there unconditionally. The future seemed far away while the past was right up close.

I was certain that somehow I would land on my feet when it was all said and done, but the anxiety of how long that might take was like a small thorn in my side. I felt a longing to go visit old places and rediscover old things. I needed to have one more "homecoming" before that term was applied to me as an alum. I needed to go home. We all want to be butterflies, but sometimes we aren't ready. That's what home is for.

My arrival to my parents house during college always consisted of being well fed by my mother, interrogated by my father, doing laundry and sleeping for approximately 12 to 14 hours.

The food at home was intoxicating. I won't bad-mouth the dining halls of my college, but nothing beats a Cuban mother's cooking. Neither the "Veggie Bar" nor "Pizza Pit" in the 1920 Commons could compare to ropa vieja (translated "old clothes," a stew of shredded flank steak in a rich tomato-based sauce) or bistec empanizado (breaded, fried steak) with white rice, black beans and fried plantains. Give me starch, give me fried and give me more! After several months away, my mother's food never tasted so delicious and my cholesterol was never so high. But, as my grandmother always said, there was no such thing as cholesterol in Cuba. So I tried to apply that theory on my short visits home. Although my father's theory of "If you eat it fast enough, your body won't know it's there" worked just as well.

After gorging myself and lazily lounging in front of a non-cable television (my father thought UHF was cable so he refused to pay extra for something we already had) in a dreamy haze from oversleeping, I called my friends to announce my arrival in the Big Apple and then was

off to experience the surreal episode that was a visit with my
grandmother.

This particular trip to Astoria where my grandmother, or Abuela,
lived was an interesting event, as usual. Abuela was my mother's mother
and a widow since my grandfather's death a year prior. My great-
grandmother had died of cancer at 33 years of age and my grandmother
spent her life believing she would die young just like her own mother.
But, she did not die young and she never let anyone forget it. When my
grandfather had been alive he joked: "She promised me when we
married that she'd die young. I'm still waiting!" Her not dying, however,
did not diminish her desire to die and it was her favorite topic of
conversation for as long as I'd known her.

My maternal grandparents came over from Cuba in 1959 just after
Castro's revolution shook the foundation of Havana. Many stayed to
reap the benefits of the uprising that soon left more people lower than
when they had begun. But citizens like my grandparents had strong ties
to the United States and the possibility of a future outside the heavy-

hand of communism. They flew out of Cuba together, unlike so many families to follow who boated, rafted and floated their way to freedom.

Transported to the new land, settling first in Tampa and then on to New York, my grandfather was able to find work as a pathologist and build himself up once again as a doctor, now in the United States. Unlike most immigrants, my grandmother was provided for well enough that she never had to enter the work force. She never had to learn English. She never wanted for anything other than her old life, her own country, and, strangely, her own death.

Her disassociation from the trials of many Cuban immigrants to the United States was only a manifestation of her true vision of herself as a Spaniard, not a Cuban. She associated herself with her roots in the Canary Islands more than she ever would with her fellow Cubans. Her beautiful Spanish features of long, straight, dark hair, dark eyes, luscious lips, and smooth olive skin only contributed more to that connotation.

But, Abuelo and Abuela were just like their fellow emigrants from Cuba in others ways: they grew old. The Abuela I knew had very little of her attractive physical features left when I knew her. Time and osteoporosis had warped her from a curvaceous beauty into a frail, hunchbacked old woman. She and my grandfather, white-haired both, watched their children grow up as they grew sicker everyday. In the spirit of my grandmother's on-going desire, Abuela prayed desperately for both of them to die, but that she go first – a race to the death, literally.

My grandmother's morbidity was hard for me to digest as a child. My parents would go out every New Year's Eve and leave my brothers and I to spend the night with Abuelo and Abuela. As they aged, the holiday grew more and more depressing as my grandmother began to use Dick Clark's *Rockin' Christmas Eve* as a countdown to her death. As we all chanted "10…9…8…" my grandmother would be audibly asking God to please take her and my grandfather before midnight so that they would not have to suffer through another year. "¡Dios mio, por favor dejame morir!" *My God, please let me die*. When she survived the passing of midnight, she'd get up as if she hadn't just been begging God to take her life, and start passing the champagne and twelve grapes we all consumed to celebrate the new year.

I comforted myself by believing that my grandmother used to be a relatively normal person. Like all butterflies, there is always evidence of the past lingering somewhere, the cocoon of the former life. My grandmother's cocoon was in her photographs, her beauty and youth frozen in time. But any questions about her youth somehow were distorted as if she did not want you to know the true story.

Her favorite photo was one taken during her honeymoon to Santiago de Cuba. I asked my grandmother why she went there on her honeymoon. She said: "Fuimos a Cuavitas porque Cheche hacia las empanadas mas deliciosas. ¿Por que preguntas? ¿Tu te vas a casar?" *We went to Cuavitas because Cheche made the most delicious empanadas* (ground meat fried inside a pocket of dough). *Why do you ask? Are you getting married?* I immediately regretted asking. My grandmother would now call several relatives and tell them I was engaged. I had once told Abuela that I did want to get married some day but that I had not yet been asked. She told

my mother that I had been proposed to by my boyfriend but I had said

no because I was thickheaded. I learned to roll with the rumors she

constantly fabricated and, after several shocking phone calls, my mother

learned to ignore the stories.

The photo I had asked about shows my grandparents in black and

white on a beach she said was called Cuavitas. My grandfather is carrying

my grandmother on his back. Despite the varying shades of gray, they

both appear tan, sprinkled wet from the ocean, their 1940s swimsuits

clinging to them. They are smiling wide with eyes twinkling of mischief.

The wedded bliss gives me a chill despite the love and youth they

project. For me the photo foreshadows a night over fifty years later

when my grandfather again carried my grandmother. He, a long time

sufferer of a heart condition, brought her wheel chair up two flights of

stairs after she landed face down in her dinner from a mild stroke. He

helped carry her into the chair and had a heart attack directly after. Two

ambulances had to come. Despite the horror and panic we went through rushing to the emergency room, we found my grandparents in beds wheeled next to one another, holding hands. My grandmother was excited about a night out. My grandfather was dying.

A few months later, my grandfather suffered his final heart attack and was perpetually freed of his longtime, painful condition. My grandmother was the loser in her morbid race to die first and her anger could not be contained. Her rage was boundless and, therefore, directed at all those around her, but most especially at God Almighty Himself.

Abuela's favorite prophecy was that she would bathe in the hot oils of hell (because she knew she'd go to hell, of course - she was a sinner and that's where she belonged) and then go directly to heaven to read the riot act to God and Saint Peter for doing this to her (don't ask me what Saint Peter's role in all this was, but I guess, as the gatekeeper, she felt he had some say in the decision to take my grandfather first). There was no quiet acceptance of her fate as part of God's plan as so many other grandmas and nanas I had met. No, for Abuela Carmelina there was no solace in the idea that she was left behind for a reason: to see her children grow and have children or to see a great-grandson be born perhaps. She was pissed and no one would hear the end of it until the end of her.

My grandmother's mourning was serious and severe and no holiday could be celebrated with her. That Easter Sunday would be no exception, hence this Saturday visit. It would be our "holiday" with her. There was no way to get her to go out anywhere because she swore she'd never go out again. In fact, her second favorite prophecy was that she would never leave the house except in a pine box on its way to be cremated. But she tolerated us being there the day before and even allowed us to bring flowers or chocolates. She loved chocolates – especially Godiva™ – despite the effect they sometimes had on her digestive system, an effect she freely spoke of quite descriptively.

I was glad to see her that afternoon despite all of this. Her demeanor became a private joke for our family, a bond only we could understand after years of exposure to her dark, cynical views. If non-Spanish speakers were with us in the presence of our grandmother, they might ask for a translation of her commentary. They would always refuse to believe that she had just said such morbid words.

My grandmother enjoyed the shock of her comments but did not like when her death was joked about. Every holiday, my grandmother would give us large gifts of money because she believed it to be her last Christmas or Easter to share with us all before she "departed." My oldest brother once dared to respond: "If you don't die, do we have to give it back?" She growled about how really this time was it, she was sure, and continued to make her announcements at every holiday that this would be her last one (although eventually she did start to cut down the amounts of our gifts). The more she rolled her eyes to heaven asking God to take her away, the more we laughed. We were used to this. What else could we do?

My father's response was always the classic one. He knew just what to say to silence my grandmother on the death topic for a few hours. He would tell her that every time she asked God to take her, He kept her alive for one more day. That infuriated her enough to keep her quiet for a while, but she was quick to rationalize: if God was really listening, then she'd already be dead. And so, on she went with her tirade.

As witnesses to this morbidity, my family was bonded in the strangest way. I could not laugh with strangers about how my grandmother was going to die…again, but I could with my brothers. Only we understood her. There was more to her too. Perhaps because, despite her demeanor, her anger was feisty, she was unmistakably alive. Somehow that inspired me. Despite all her talk of death, she was still a survivor. She was still our heritage. She was still part of us.

After collecting our chocolates and flowers and lamenting her old age, my grandmother stoically announced that it was time for us to leave or else "die in the traffic" going home. Despite never having driven, she was an expert on the rail and road report. And so ended our visit. There would be many more days like that with Abuela in my future. That thought alone brought on anxiety. Thank God it was Saturday night.

Easter Morning

I hadn't been drinking enough to be hung over on Easter morning, but I wasn't feeling energetic either. I watched some boring television, the plague of not having cable, and then decided to start the laundry. It would take more than a few hours to get through the bundle I had brought home from college, not to mention the small surprise that I found when I got down to the basement

While many chastise America's college students for lazily dragging home their laundry, no one comments on the even bigger sinners: the parents who wait until the kids get home to change their bed linen, replace the towels in the bathroom and launder all their ironable items. My one or two washes that morning became hours of folding, ironing and hanging. Most of my laundry consisted of jeans, t-shirts and flannel shirts (yes, this was college fashion) specifically geared so I wouldn't have to iron. Therefore, it was almost guaranteed that most of the items I had to "pay special attention to" were not my own.

Finally, there was time for a break and I began to flip through old photo albums in the basement as I waited for the dryer to stop. There were many vacation pictures highlighting trips, people and outfits I barely remembered. My hair was short, then long; I was in sailor suits and bathing suits; standing by palm trees then fir trees. Throughout, I was tan and smiling. I looked at my own hands in comparison as I turned the pages of the albums. They were eerily pale from a long winter spent inside libraries, classrooms and college bars.

Then there were the school albums: my oldest brother, Kevin, in high school with the feathered hair of the late 70's hanging over his ears and an outfit consisting of an array of browns and tans. My middle brother, Michael, in a grammar school uniform of a yellow shirt and a dark green tie with the initials "AS" for All Saints School. (Curiously, they never went ahead and put "ASS" on the ties, which I thought would add much-needed humor to our surroundings.) His light brown hair was slicked to the side and pressed firmly against his head, my mother's technique I was sure, and on his face a big, toothy grin.

And me, the youngest, in a pale blue dress on my first day of kindergarten. My hair was long and straight with bangs. I was holding my mom's hand as we stood right outside the entrance. The sun was shining. My mom was blond with wavy hair in the photo. I looked extremely happy to be going to school. I guess attitudes don't change much. I was always happy to go to school. But how everything else had changed!

First of all, my mom is not blond. Never has been except for that one tango with Miss Clairol, captured forever on film. She is a natural brunette, although the real color may have been lost to years of tampering. But her natural hue is captured in her eyes: the dark, chocolate eyes of my grandmother in a face much more round atop a body that is somewhat short and heavy but one that demands to be hugged when you walk through the door.

After the 70's, Kevin's brown's hair never grew to be more than an inch long and he wouldn't be caught dead in any shade of brown or tan. Even though his company became business casual long ago, he remains corporate in his medium height, firm build and painfully gripping handshake. On the other hand, Michael's smooth, side-brushed hair has been sticking up wildly with a vengeance since the late 80's. Now there is a small chip in that big grin that happened soon after the photo was taken. It softens his features, much like the weight around the middle that has now become a part of his gentle nature.

And then there's my father, or Papa, I should say. He is the same in every photo, from the wedding portrait taken not long after his arrival from Cuba to our recent holiday snapshots. With his thin stature now rounded out in the center, his dark brown hair graying on the sideburns, his thick-framed glasses thinning out to contemporary frames, his biggish nose, his smile and his expression are timeless; a pillar in the family album. Never trendy. The classic dad.

It is amazing how we all drifted from what we used to be, but our essence remained the same. Photos don't capture everything, but sometimes they capture more than we think: how my brothers share my dad's lip-biting grin or how my mom and I have the same thoughtful eyes. It's all there in a photo waiting to be noticed: the essence of the butterfly, the humbleness of the caterpillar; small, beautiful characteristics easy to miss unless you really are looking.

And I was looking. I examined closely the pictures of my father. Has he even aged? "Your dad is 60?" people ask in disbelief. He sure is, but it's impossible to tell. His hair has barely grayed and he is as strong and energetic as ever (when he chooses to be) and mentally he's on the ball. The signs of aging are his long-winded stories, which get quirkier and quirkier as time goes on and his increasing expenditures on Lotto. As I sat in the basement flipping through albums, I hear him in the kitchen playing a scratch game. He must've searched for hours to find a place to buy it on Easter Sunday.

I continued to look even though the dryer had stopped. The pictures from when I was younger are comical. The ones from when I was older were just embarrassing. It's as if I became a teenager and tried too hard to look a certain way. I lost that innocence. The excitement of just being in a picture wasn't good enough. By the time I got to the high school albums, I could tell no photo was taken without at least ten minutes of preparation. They were interesting to see, but I liked the older albums better.

Kindergarten was a great time to look at. The young, shining faces in a brightly colored classroom. Little hands holding crayons and looking sticky from cookies and juice. Who would get to pull the cookie wagon that day? Who would lead the group in the pledge of allegiance? It was a time of honor and special privileges; of friendship and young love. A time when Halloween was magical and Christmas was real. Holidays were made up of candy and presents and that was okay because we were too young to know what materialism was all about even though it was our lifestyle.

As I flipped through more kindergarten photos, I came across one in particular that struck me. Faces forgotten until that moment and suddenly a flood of recognition of names and places and incidents came over me. Four of us seated at the small blue pastel table in my kindergarten classroom at All Saints School. In the photo, it is

Halloween and we are all in costume. I am dressed like an angel, grinning from ear to ear. I loved to dress up that way even other days of the year that weren't necessarily costume-related, much to the chagrin of my older brothers who had to face the embarrassment of being seen with me in public.

I was obsessed with angels, the beauty and mystery of them. These were beings with huge fluffy wings that flew into the sky and had a regular dialogue with God. Angels had beautiful glowing halos just like their colleagues in the *Picture Book of Saints*. To be honest, I was uncertain of the difference between saints and angels but knew their halos in common were significant. I imagined a halo as being some type of communicator with God, like an antenna attached to the head for easy listening.

Failing to understand the hardships of what the saints went through, I idolized them, wanted to be like them. I wanted to mimic St. Agnes whose hands and wrists were so small that the Roman chains slipped off her arms; St. Barbara locked in her tower; or, St. George fighting dragons. The lives of the saints were better than any episode of *Super Friends*. To me, saints were like cartoon characters. Saints, angels, fairies, pixies, Tinker Bell, Mickey Mouse. It all made sense in a Disney/Hanna Barbara sort of way. My whole belief system bounced between *The Adventures of Scooby Doo* and *My First Holy Bible*. No wonder I was confused. Other girls dressed up like princesses and movie stars. I was wearing a rosary as costume jewelry trying to take flight with mesh wings. Luckily, I was still at an age where the kids around me barely noticed.

In the photograph of the four of us sitting at the kindergarten table, only part of the kindergarten classroom was visible in the background. The edges of the red and brown cardboard playhouse where the girls pretended to tend house were barely visible. I remembered the boys raiding us every five minutes screaming "Terrorist commandos!" and torturing our innocent dolls. They secretly just wanted to see what we were doing inside the playhouse and we secretly loved them coming in and interrupting our boring games of house.

The photo also showed the lower portion of the shelves in the back of the classroom that held our sunflowers planted in small paper cups. I briefly searched for but could not find the photograph of my full-grown sunflower that had almost become the size of a tree. It was my one and only successful botanical endeavor. To this day, I believe my parents bought a sunflower and planted it in place of my own dying seed.

Despite the hundreds of photos of my childhood years, I was drawn back to the kindergarten Halloween photo again and again. In it, I'm seated together with José Toledo dressed as Tron, Greg Riccola as Batman and Francis Laboure as Dracula. Seeing Greg and José sitting together so happily struck me as unusual. Their chumminess barely lasted until the next year when the two had a huge fallout over a box of chocolates. Like I said, materialism was our lifestyle. The story goes something like this:

In the great tradition of Catholic School slave labor, which includes clapping erasers, having to fetch the janitor from the dungeon that was the school basement and unloading and distributing textbooks for lazy teachers who had better things to do behind the heavy door of the smoke-filled faculty lounge, came the fundraiser.

My particular favorite was the chocolate sale. The All Saints' candy bars were long, rectangular chocolates wrapped in foil covered with a white band. Each bar's wrapper held inside the precious McDonald's coupon for a free hamburger. The purpose of the fundraiser was to have every student sell at least one box of chocolate. Our incentive was the distinguished honor of not having to wear a uniform for one day. I looked forward to this glorious occasion for weeks, only to forget and wear my uniform that day anyway. It probably didn't matter much since the devious administration would usually make dress-down day a half-day so as to remove as much pleasure from our lives as possible.

In my family, the fundraiser consisted of various family members pilfering most of the chocolate and my mother finding out. She would yell and scream at my father as she wrote a check to the school. He would stoically take the blame and we would all be happy. It was a tradition we celebrated annually. Greg's family was different.

The Riccola's believed in the fundraiser and pushed chocolate onto family, friends, clients, postal employees – anyone who wouldn't go into a diabetic coma anytime soon was fair game. So Greg would sell out and come to school every other day requesting more chocolate. When the school secretary entered our classroom with another box of chocolate for Greg, whispering and fidgeting ceased as a strange hush overcame the room.

One day, the box was delivered just as we returned from gym class and began to put on our uniforms, as was custom, on top of our gym clothes. I believe the rationale for not allowing the students to change in the bathroom where they would be able to remove their gym clothes and put on their regular uniforms had to do with losing them forever in the unsupervised stalls of the bathroom. Send five or more girls to the restroom, and you were never sure when they would return. So, we performed the strange ritual of getting dressed in front of one another. In the air lingered the strange post-gym buzz and energy that usually lasted the entire afternoon. The box of chocolate sitting on Greg's desk only added to that excitement.

Despite the fact that all the boxes of chocolate were the same ones each and every student received at the start of this seemingly endless fundraiser, each new box brought insatiable curiosity as to its contents. On this day in particular, probably hyped up from gym class, José pushed things a step too far. Everyone stared as he, shirt still half-opened revealing his gym shirt underneath, asked to *see* the box.

Now, "see" in first grade really meant, "Can I put my hands all over your stuff? Huh? Huh? Can I? Can I? Pleeeeease." So, understandably, Greg replied with a curt no. I mean, this was his family's chocolate. Why would he want José's sweaty gym hands man-handling his sweets, the key to not only dress down days but endless cool prizes from the prize book?

But, José persisted and further denial gave him no other recourse but to make a bold move: he reached toward the box to "see" anyway.

Greg pushed José off to protect his precious chocolates but in the struggle José swung at him with his "instant" tie. Who could forget that ingenious invention? Designed for the six-year-old who could never tie his own tie and still make it to school on time, and for a Catholic institution that would never allow male students to go without ties, the "instant" tie was the perfect solution. It had a small latch that hooked beneath the shirt collar giving the semblance of a tied tie without the hassle of the real thing.

The small hook that tied the tie is what landed in Greg's scalp and it was José's yank that caused enough blood for Greg to be taken to the hospital. It also caused enough of an uproar for José to be severely punished (no dress-down day, probably). The memory of the incident, which may have been easily forgotten by the boys themselves, was kept alive by bitter parents who years later were still angry over the "Chocolate Incident." But despite the violence, the chocolate sales waged on, Greg maintaining his excessive lead despite the injury. Although, I do remember that in subsequent years, José himself became a top chocolate salesman. I'm not sure if the incidents were related, but they might have been.

I had to laugh at the silliness of it in retrospect. I wonder how José and Greg saw it. Could they laugh at it now or do they maintain a grudge? Do they still tell the story in anger, perhaps to their own children? Do they even remember, like I do, Greg's return to school with the bandage on his head, the delicious forbidden taste of the All Saints' chocolate or the impending excitement of dress-down day that really was never as good as it was built up to be?

As I continued to stare at the photo, at my own young face beneath dark, straight bangs, I found myself overwhelmed with a strange sense of melancholy. Francis' face in that picture instilled sadness in me despite his large smile and bright blue eyes. It might not have been evident to someone else glancing at the old photo, but to me, knowing what happened to Francis, seeing him dressed as Dracula, with his cape like a black shroud creeping up on my own shoulder, it seemed ominous. We all seemed so happy but his innocence was tragic to me.

I wondered why he had been singled out on his birthday. Why had his party been so unsuccessful? I felt compelled to tell him that I thought he was a nice kid. I wanted to make sure that he wasn't still sad about it, that he was okay with it. I wanted to reach out to him. I couldn't help but wonder: whatever happened to Francis Laboure?

Suddenly, the doorbell snapped my attention away from the album and into the dingy basement. I heard a kitchen chair scrape the floor as my dad rose to answer it. My brother, Michael, had arrived. I pulled the photo from the book and tucked it in a folded shirt I was taking back to school with me. I had the entire bus ride back to Philly to mull over the past and the possible outcomes of Francis' life. Perhaps he too was now a butterfly and I had only known him as the worm. It was the Spring. Anything was possible.

<u>Commencement</u>

A large meal and hours of folding clothes later, I was back on the bus headed to school in Philadelphia for the final stretch of senior year at college. The longtime victim of motion sickness, I found myself unable to read. I was forced to recount my brief time at home and all that lay ahead in the next few weeks. The morbid visit with my grandmother was typically surreal and the Easter meal with my family was certainly memorable, but it was the time in the basement that was heaviest on my mind. This irretrievable past alive only in photo albums and memories was trapped in my head waiting to emerge in a better form. It was nice to hide in the memories and faces of long ago when the future was somewhat daunting.

The kindergarten photograph was the epitome of a better time for me, a time when my education was just beginning and I had a long road ahead. Now that road was slowly coming to an end and I was not sure what would or could happen next.

Despite my excitement to finish the term and graduate, I was dreading the moment, attaching negative thoughts whenever I could. I envisioned my graduation gown having the same effect as Francis' cape in that Halloween photo, being this dark ominous symbol that made me want to curl up in thoughts of the past and not face the future. We would graduate in black robes, a dark sea of bodies forming a great shadow that would float over Franklin Football Field on a hot summer day. Banners, balloons, flashbulbs of light would celebrate the event, but the procession of dark figures was ominous in my mind, like a funeral march with Pomp and Circumstance as the dirge.

Beyond that day the future was uncertain. Some of my peers had jobs, some had new schools to attend, others had prospects, but many of us had nothing. I was scared. Our commencement speech, given by Bill Cosby, did nothing to allay that fear. "The Cos" didn't really make us laugh as he did in so many episodes of *The Cosby Show*. He spoke to us about how we could not enter the working world believing the world owed us something. We had to work hard and prove ourselves. Our education gave us an advantage but not a privilege. I realized I was secretly counting on the latter and the dream was coming to an end.

I was a student since I was four years old, an individual defined by the academic setting: extracurriculars, classes, relationships to other students and teachers. Even summer jobs were framed by my inevitable return to school at the end of vacation.

In the academic progression, I was a student passed along from grade to grade with recommendations and words of good will from the previous teacher. So, my work was always judged in comparison to past projects and my grades scaled above or below what I "was capable of," an undefined criteria. From grammar school to high school, there were transcripts and recommendations and from high school to college, even more so. Although the level of education was higher, we were still dealing with the same world, the same profession. Basically, I had proven myself once in pre-Kindergarten by performing the "Hokey Pokey" correctly and ever since my teachers seemed to refer to that great past accomplishment.

How do you leap from that type of safe, accepting environment to a job? An employer would see right through my résumé and probably not give a damn about my Hokey-Pokey triumphs of prior years. There could be no hiding behind a Catholic school uniform or an A in Language Arts (strong Phonics just doesn't go as far as it used to). It would now be relevant experience, a foot in the door and a finger on the pulse of the industry. About all I had was my name on several important-looking pieces of paper, a solid GPA and expert knowledge of how to walk into a crowded bar and be served a drink within five minutes.

I had no recourse. No job. No plans. No direction. Part of it was not my fault. The communications industry was distinct in its demand that you be "ready to work tomorrow" before you applied for a job. My every inquiry was deferred as I was told to get in touch again when I got to New York. So I was forced to wait and see. That was the painful part but it kept me going from one day to the next.

I made it through graduation. I made it through the packing and selling and moving and driving. I made it through a trip to Ireland and back again. And in the end, I ended up back in my dark, damp basement with no interviews lined up, only one single job offer from a firm back in Philadelphia and a photo album on my lap, begging me to remember.

The Unwritten

In second grade, Mrs. Carlos had given us the assignment to write a poem. I have searched high and low for that piece of paper hoping to capture the excitement, spirit and mischievousness of those few rhyming lines, but I never have. I was so proud of what I had written and Mrs. Carlos had seemed so excited about it. I was beaming with pride. It had felt magical to write something. I was fixated on the concept of being able to take an idea, a mere thought, write it down and have someone else understand it without my saying a word.

That was second grade, the year of my first poem. The year I learned to write script. I wrote poems in script, all curly and slanted. It was the beginning of my love affair with writing. I kept a serious diary for my entire childhood, wrote poems for every occasion, stories for every creative writing assignment. Up until high school, I felt that I had a gift.

In my freshman year of high school, my intense and sophisticated English teacher told our class that there was a poetry contest and if anyone wanted to enter, they should let her know. After class one day, I mustered the courage to tell her that I wrote poetry and she asked me if I had any of my work with me. I took out my small, red, cloth-covered notebook with handwritten poems that were drenched with lovesick teen verses and silly rhymes but that also housed some poetry that I was actually proud of. Before I could explain that I wanted to recopy a few poems onto loose paper, she snatched the book and said she'd look it over. I was forced to exit the room mortified but excited at the prospect that a real literary person was going to review my poems.

Later in the week, she asked me to stay after class. When I got to her desk, she handed me back my book of poems without looking at me and began to pack up her briefcase. She told me that what I had given her was trash and there was nothing in there she believed was worth submitting for the contest. To this day, I force myself to believe that she was not aware of what she was saying or that perhaps I misheard her. I don't know. But I rarely showed anyone my poems again. And if I did, no matter how much they were praised, I felt that the reader was lying to cover up the truth. In college I met too many others who were poets and authors and I felt that my work amounted to very little compared to theirs. In fact, I slowly began to hide that part of me and, eventually, I stopped writing creatively altogether.

That kindergarten photo of Francis that I found in my basement did more for me than just show me a different time; it made me remember a feeling that I had long ago forgotten. It revived in me a longing for something that I once thought was talent but that I had forced myself to hide. That photo had sparked a longing for that time again. Not just childhood, but unabashed desire to create something beautiful and meaningful, to be proud of my work. My indecision and reluctance to aggressively search for a real job was perhaps that I wasn't sure a regular position could offer me that type of satisfaction. I was no longer sure of what I wanted.

And then I was. I wanted to recreate that time in my childhood again. I wanted to know seven again. I wanted to write about it or write about looking for it. I wanted to write about searching and write about writing about searching. I wanted to say to the world it was okay to not know what you want and turn the idea of that into something meaningful. But I wanted more.

I wanted to reconnect with the past. I wanted to have a reunion. I wanted to hold hands with all the old kids and play dodge ball again. I wanted to wear my gym uniform under my clothes and sell chocolate up and down my street. I wanted to find out how things were at All Saints when I transferred out in fourth grade. What happened to each of them in the long progress of their lives? I wanted to know if they were as mixed up as I was, if they remembered Mrs. Sinow's wig. I wanted to know what really happened to Francis.

There was so much going on in my heart, I wanted to find the root of all that feeling and pass it along. I wanted to rediscover my talent. I wanted to share my talent. I wanted to make something good out of the not knowing, out of the little direction I had.

Staring at that picture gave me the idea for the first step. I wanted to write a book. I had no idea how to go about writing one, what it would take to fulfill the endeavor or whether or not I had the talent to make it any good, but the storyline was simple enough and I was willing to give it a try: I was going to find Francis.

My goal was to look for this person and write a book about the experience. Through the process I would tell the story of myself, tell the story of what it is to be a young, struggling writer trying to find herself. It would be easy.

Then came the complication: putting pen to paper. How on earth would I start this epic search? The logistics seemed strangely simple: the phone book. But, when I did find him, what would I possibly have to say to him? That's when I started to worry.

Then again, the idea had possibilities. I mean, I was single. What if he was single? We could make babies or something and I could write a book about each baby as sequels. *Finding Francis Jr.* No, that idea was strangely repulsive. But, sadly, I knew it could sell.

I would start simply and easily. I went to a small stationary store that over the years had become more of a Lotto stronghold than anything else. There I found a black and white marble composition notebook of the likes I had when I was in first and second grade. It was made of cardboard and in my hands felt sturdy and strong. I paid 99 cents for that notebook. It could have gotten fancier but I wanted to be as straightforward as I could. I wanted to be basic and firm. No bells and whistles. Just me and my writing.

Next, I dug out my class picture from first grade. In this photograph, the rows of All Saints first-graders were neatly pressed in their uniforms and Mrs. Sinow standing behind us, serious and stern. I took the photo to a copy store and had a color copy made. I pasted that photo to the front of my notebook for inspiration.

I went to my bedroom, lay back into the pillows and thought about my words. I opened the notebook to reveal its startling white pages with their thin, blue, horizontal lines and long, red margins down the left side. The surface was clean and smooth. I ran my hand along that first page many times, warming it to my touch, imagining how I would start my story.

I was finally ready to begin.

<u>All Saints</u>

At this point in time, my immediate goal was to find Francis Laboure and write about that experience. Everything else that happened along the way was just more fodder for me. I had already tried the modern modes of locating someone: the phone book and the Internet. I won't say that I didn't find the name Francis Laboure. I did. My problem was that I found too many. I called every one located in New York City but couldn't begin to hope to call all the names I found on the Internet from all over the country. So I decided to back away from the conventional approach until I had discovered some more information.

It was time to start digging. I was ready to sink my teeth into some real detective work. I was finally ready for this challenge. Well, actually, I was looking for anything that would get me out of the house. The midday sun along with the excruciating daytime plot of *Days of Our Lives* slowly started to make my head hurt. This mental state lent itself perfectly to the idea of a field trip. I got dressed up and prepared myself for a real adventure. I selected the destination and plotted out how to get there. I was traveling to my old grammar school, All Saints. It would take two buses to get there and on a sluggish summer afternoon it would certainly take some time, at least enough time for me to think of what I was getting myself into.

I was four years old when I began at the All Saints' School. I had started in the Catholic version of pre-Kindergarten called "Prayer School." We did everything the other Pre-K kids did, but with our own religious twist. We colored pictures, but ours were of angels. We sang and danced, but a majority of our songs were about God and Jesus. "This Little Light of Mine" and "He's Got the Whole World in His Hands" were popular tunes. Sister Helen presided over our small class taught in a room inside the convent, across the street from the church and elementary school of All Saints.

As the second bus of my day approached the school, I felt strangely sad. I was nostalgiac for my childhood, that feeling somewhere in my toes, a struggle between wanting to be a bigger kid, but loving the games and toys of my own age. I was saddened also by the harsh reality of the memory that many bad things happened between the time I was four years old attending prayer school and the day my family withdrew me from All Saints.

As the bus slowed down, I looked at the building that used to be the convent, now someone's home? I wasn't sure. I knew it had been sold in conjunction with the old rectory to pay for the new rectory, something of a mansion that now stands beside the dusty tan church. Its diarrheal color made my stomach hurt as I stepped off the bus and passed the convent.

The nuns, Sister Helen, Sister Margaret and Sister Nicola, were now long gone too. These were old, strong women of God who watched helplessly as their home was sold in order to raise revenue for the luxurious new home for the parish priests. Despite the protests among the congregation and the parents of students attending the schools, the nuns were not provided or offered any place of their own. Also, because it was against the church doctrine for priests and nuns to share a living space, the elderly women were forced to leave the parish.

Retirement at the motherhouse far out in Long Island saved Sister Helen, but nothing could save Sister Margaret who died of cancer soon after the incident far away from what had been her home and parish for many years. Barely anyone knew that she had died since most of the families had pulled their children out of All Saints by the time the new rectory's foundation had been dug. Those families never returned to the parish. They all had their reasons.

For some it was the controversy of the construction, the amount of money being spent, which seemed to contradict the vows of poverty the priests had taken. For others, it was the more serious irony that while nuns and priests were not allowed to share a living space in the rectory, the two priests, Father Daly and Father Peters, who resided together, were lovers. Then there was the alcoholism of Father Peters that brought him to the point of verbal abusiveness to several parishioners. But by the time news of all of this emerged, no one cared because most of the children were nestled softly in another local parish in Bayside, Sister Helen was legally blind, and All Saints almost bankrupt.

It seemed a disappointment that after all the protests and the words about God's love no one cared. But it was true. People had to move on. Church scandals were par for the course. Even my mom became jaded to the experience. Perhaps she had the most reason.

We had been caroling the Christmas before we left the parish and when we stopped at the rectory Father Daly took my mother into his glass-walled office to have a "talk" about the families protesting the new construction. The next thing I knew, I saw Father Daly raise a hand to strike my mother. He didn't strike but it hovered there waiting for her to say something that just might bring it to her face. My mother did not look scared. She looked tired. Perhaps she was just another member of a generation that had seen the most abusive aspects of the Catholic Church. Perhaps she had seen Father Daly do this before. She let him have his say. Eventually his hand came down, slowly, reluctantly landing by his side.

Someone said Father Daly was drunk and, in retrospect, he must have been because any sober person would know that the person he should've been angry with was Agnes DiBenedetto, not my mom. It was Agnes who told the other parents that she "knew people" who could "do things." No one understood exactly what that meant but we imagined it had something to do with the windows in the new rectory being smashed every time new ones were put in.

I thought my mom was pretty tactful about not bringing up Agnes that night or even years later when Father Peter called her to make his peace about all that had happened. She merely responded to his desire to make peace with God by saying that, because of him, she couldn't make her own peace with God and then she hung up the phone.

My mom is one of the strongest people I know. Father Peters was not and he died weeks later of complications from pneumonia. No one cared. No one even remembered him by then. But I did. I remembered it all as I stood on the corner no longer facing All Saints but the building across the street, the building that used to be the old rectory, the building where Father Daly shook an angry fist at my mother while all the kids stood around wide-eyed wondering whether or not he'd hit her and why when we were supposed to be Christmas caroling. We weren't doing anything wrong. I remember seeing Baby Jesus in the manger by the door looking at me sadly, asking me "Why?" as if I knew.

Now the rectory sign has been replaced with a larger one reading "Gynecology and Obstetrics." I laughed because I knew from the papers how the priests who now live in the new rectory want to take that sign down more than anything. They want no one to know that behind the new sign on the old rectory, sold in a mad rush to get money for the lavish new rectory's construction, non-Catholic doctors perform abortions on young Catholic women in the shadow of a brick church called All Saints.

As the bus pulled away and I began to approach my old grammar school, I realized something I would never forget: it was in this place that I knew Francis. It was in these halls that the innocents were educated, amidst educators who were not so innocent. I had no idea.

Was there a dark reason behind Francis' birthday party and sudden departure? Was his family involved in the controversy early on? What other sins hid within the walls of All Saints?

My years at All Saints represented a time when I believed in the saints, when I believed in their miracles and stories. I believed in virtue and suffering for a greater purpose, a fundamental concept that I carried with me all my life: we suffer for a purpose. We have to. Bad things happen for a reason. Now being older, seeing more of the world, I was no longer certain of that even though I wanted so much to know that again, have my heart tell me so.

Standing on that corner I saw in All Saints my need to find Francis, my need to discover that the bad thing that happened to him as a child happened for a reason. To find out why he left, to find him was to find out that there was hope for me amid all the confusion. I came back to All Saints to find hope and renew my faith in life's purpose, my purpose. I came back to All Saints for Francis but, also, I came back to All Saints for me.

The Visitation

"I'm not afraid of you. I'm not afraid," I repeated to myself after I rang the doorbell of the elementary school. All Saints' secretaries were infamous for being rude, obnoxious and condescending…to adults. They were believed to eat small children. As a young woman, I feared falling prey again to severe looks and reprimands and backing down from my mission.

My initial phone call had uncovered nothing except that things never change: I was berated for asking such an inappropriate question and mocked for not looking the name up in the phone book. "Save yourself the trouble," were the words she used, as if I hadn't tried that already days before and failed miserably. I was told that regardless of whether or not they could help me, any request would have to be made in person. So, they wouldn't just say no over the phone. You'd have to get down there in person for them to say it to your face.

I hung up the phone terrified of the prospect but suddenly certain this gave me an advantage.

"I am not afraid of you. I am not afraid," I kept repeating, waiting to hear footsteps coming down the stairs. But enough time had gone by and I felt justified to ring again. There were cars in the parking lot and I was there during regular office hours so I was sure someone would answer.

The door finally opened. I recognized the face: old, wrinkled and overdone in outlandish makeup that went well with her garish costume jewelry. She had been the receptionist since Sister Teresa died sixteen years earlier, but I had never learned her name.

She looked at me and I saw bitterness, but of what I wasn't sure. She looked me up and down and I realized there was a faint glimmer of recognition in her eyes. I was sure she was remembering who I was, who my family was, why we had left the parish so long ago. She had the angry appearance of the soldier who, after being left behind on the battlefield, later runs into a member of the troop that had deserted. There was the wild look of the competent left too long in the insane asylum.

These observations were a great exaggeration of the simple fact that either she remembered me and had disliked my mother (not completely out of the question) or that this woman was irritated by my stopping by on a summer afternoon. Either way, I was a nuisance and she wasn't going to let me inside.

"You don't have to keep ringing the bell. I heard you the first time," she complained.

"I wasn't sure if anyone was here, if anyone heard…"

"I heard. Now what do you want?" she snapped. My powers were fading. She obviously didn't notice my beautiful eggplant-colored interview suit.

"I called earlier this week. I am searching for a former classmate."

"Oh well. I see. I don't think we can help you." I felt my blood pressure rise as she began to close the door. I stuck my hand out.

"But I called and spoke to you and you told me to come. That's why I'm here. At least let me in." I felt anger rising and she sensed it. She opened the door further and let me pass her to step inside. The building was dark and cool within. There was a faint odor of stale sandwich bread and ammonia. I felt nausea begin to build.

We walked up one flight of stairs to where the principal's office was located. It was adjacent to the first grade classroom where I had my classes with Francis and Mrs. Sinow. I suddenly felt I had come to the right place. This visit seemed "right" despite the resistance I was encountering.

It dawned on me why the first-grade class was infamously well-behaved when we were left unattended by our teacher: we were terrified of the principal being a stone's throw away, frightened of her wrath. The principal I was about to meet was not the same woman we had feared but she had the same title and I was about to face her. My nausea worsened. Perhaps it wasn't too late to leave.

It was. I was now face to face with the school's current principal: Sister Mary Somethingorother. Her extreme girth startled me and I didn't quite catch her name. I did immediately get the point she was making: there was no way I'd be able to review Francis Laboure's records and find out where he mysteriously transferred after first grade.

I had just begun this search and it seemed I had already failed, but not completely. Sister Mary Whatever did say, statistically speaking, that most transfers ended up at Public School 66. I smiled and wrote "P.S. 66" into my notepad, trying to remain as professional as possible as I thanked her. There was not much left to say so I attempted to leave but the witch-like receptionist insisted on escorting me out. I thought she might have something to say but she remained silent so I deduced that she was merely preventing me from performing any acts of vandalism or stealing valuable chalk from an unlocked classroom. Alumni of All Saints were obviously not regarded highly. Either way, I was happy to escape. The door was slammed sharply behind me as I stepped boldly into the hot June sunshine.

I hadn't lost this battle but I hadn't exactly won either. I had a vague lead and an even vaguer idea of where this project was going. I walked down the street thinking of what direction to take but quickly ended up on the bus back home.

Dead End

I returned home and mistakenly waited until the next day before I put a call in to P.S. 66. As I dialed I looked at the calendar and realized the timing of this call might not be to my advantage. School was already over but it was dangerously near the day school offices would close for the summer. I surmised that tired administrative assistants would not be anxious to hear questions whose answers were not simply yes or no.

Coming straight out of university life, it was surprising to me that a record could not be pulled from an accessible file or quickly verified at the touch of a button. Obviously this was not the case with All Saints and would certainly not be the case in a small public school in Queens. Even less likely was the idea that whatever information was obtained could be given via telephone the day before P.S. 66's office was to close for the summer. I had been right: my timing was atrocious.

The young woman who answered the phone told me I would have to go there in person before they closed that day to have my question even considered.

"Our office doesn't close until one so you have time."

I looked at the digital clock on the microwave and it read 12:30. Fat chance. I had no car and would have to take a minimum of two buses to make it there. I had also only gotten up in time to see the end of "The Price is Right" so a shower would certainly be a necessary activity as well. I didn't tell her that I was talking to her in my Garfield nightgown, but I did tell her it would be impossible for me to come down to the office that day. Before I could even offer to go the next day, she told me to try again in September and hung up the phone.

I mumbled an ungrateful thank-you into the whining dial tone and hung up the receiver. I was not a truly religious person at this point in my life, but I quickly accepted that this was a sign from God telling me to give up. If I was meant to find hope, if I was meant to find Francis, the path would be clearer. After thinking this, I knew I was quitting. I had never realized how easy it was to throw in the towel. As I ran upstairs to my room to put on my bathing suit and gear up for an afternoon of "Days of Our Lives" and sunbathing, I continued to convince myself how it was time to put this entire idea to rest.

Even if I did find Francis, I might uncover something I didn't want to know. He could be dead or badly crippled in an accident. He could be in prison, on drugs or both. He could be an alcoholic or a child abuser. What if he was clinically depressed or certifiably insane? What if he was a circus freak or a serial killer? He could embody the opposite of hope, the opposite of positive meaning in suffering. Why would I want to find that?

Or what if he wasn't? What if he was okay? A swinging single? Married? A father of one? Two? Three even?? A good son to his mother? A professional? In graduate school? A factory worker? A waiter? A writer? What if he had moved on? What if he didn't remember this whole birthday party memory I had placed so much importance on? And who was I to remind him of that day?

As I squirmed into my suit, I realized that this whole idea was crazy. If I actually found him, where would we go from there? Would I confront him? Would I give him a business card and ask him to keep in touch? How would I relate what could only be taken as an obsession with his past? How would I tell him all of this without frightening him or without making him think I was crazy? How could I tell someone that my idea for a book focused on an event years ago without making him feel I've trivialized a part of his life? How do I stand before him, open my mouth and expect words to come out when I really have nothing to say to him? What if he realizes it isn't about him? What if he realizes that it's about me? It is about me.

I sat down on the bed in my bathing suit and took a deep breath. I looked out of the window at the sun shining through the tree in front of my house and remembered that I had never climbed it. I remembered my brother climbing it and that every time he did, I wanted to go up there and couldn't. Each time he got to a higher branch, I cared less that he was up there and more that I wasn't. It was about me when he climbed the tree even though it was him that was climbing. I was the one left behind wondering why.

This was about me, my path, my world and the role Francis Laboure had once played in it a long time ago. How do I remind him about what may have been the worst day of his life and not admit that I'm using that one day, one afternoon, as a catalyst for a search into myself, a search to understand myself as a writer? I couldn't.

I grabbed a towel and my sunglasses and slowly walked downstairs to distract myself from what I was reluctant to face at that moment. That my search was not worth all the painful things I might uncover about this person. I could not go on.

The Path is Chosen

After my visit to All Saints, I stopped writing. I put away the black and white marble composition notebook with a color-copied photo of All Saints class taped to the front and began packing. In the same week that I decided to write a book, I gave it up and took the only job offer I received after graduation from a small advertising agency in Philadelphia. The only thing worse in my mind than doing something I didn't care about was not having money to pay my bills and subsisting off of my parents for the next few years. I decided to take the job and put the book aside for now. I actually believed I could take a break for a few years, get my career going and then eventually come back to it. It seemed very easy. Perhaps a little bit too easy. But I was not inclined to fight it.

And the more I thought about it, the more I realized that my book idea was an exciting concept but difficult to pin down. Who would want to read this soul-searching epic? How would I go about introducing a reader into my life? It was harder and harder to imagine presenting myself as a full-time writer, let alone an author. This wasn't something my friends were doing, this wasn't something they were into. They might even laugh at the notion. I mean, the book idea was really from left field. No one had a clue.

I did not consider my decision to stop writing the book a failure because I hadn't told anyone that I was going to write one in the first place. If it failed or never got written, no one would know about it. And, if it was successful, I could tell anyone I wanted about it. But for right now, Francis was going to be my secret. Eventually, I would take my time and enjoy finding him, enjoy the process of writing, but for now there was no need to let on to what was not happening.

I moved forward with the knowledge that I already had a path, finally had a job and the need for the search was no longer. I had hope. I didn't need to pick away at the past when the future was so bright. I really didn't need Francis or this book to fulfill me. My life was fun and happy. To celebrate that fact, I called all my friends together to have a goody-bye happy hour. It was time to celebrate a new beginning that had nothing to do with Francis Laboure.

Happy Hour

Happy hour was probably a lot happier for me than it was for anyone else. I had just gotten home and my family and friends were curious as to my quick turnaround back out of New York State. My friends at least could be upfront about it and say they were sad to see me leave and expressed hope that I'd visit often. My parents are not as straightforward. They believed whole-heartedly in brainwashing. They almost won.

The first level of attack was physical: There was criticism about how often or little I bathed; I was either wasting water or going to die from being dirty. I received speeches on why I was going to die because I refused to sleep with the air conditioner on. I heard lectures for leaving the house with my hair wet despite the tropical temperature that summer in Queens. The outcome, of course, was death. It seemed my mother had picked up my grandmother's taste for the morbid and I had to keep reminding her that it was a bit over the top.

But I knew none of it was real. It was all a cover of Cuban melodrama to conceal the underlying issue, the most pressing concern: I was ruining my life and I was doing it by leaving home…again. College was one thing but returning to Philadelphia after college was ridiculous. After the hoopla of leaving Philadelphia, after moving all my stuff back into our house, I was now doing the exact opposite of what I had set out to do. To argue why that was suddenly okay was difficult.

At first I tried to convince them, but it was hard to do seeing that I myself was not completely convinced. Finally I gave up and stood by one reason, the one concrete thing that most people will nod at when you mention, that both parents and grandparents can understand, the same I used when choosing the college I attended: I was offered good money.

It wasn't a lie. Potenta actually offered a better salary than what I had been offered in a pathetic handful of interviews in New York City. Plus, with a lower cost of living, I would be able to subsist just fine. I knew that by being economical I sounded more sensible, but not necessarily convincing. To my parents, I had almost immediately given up on New York because one quick job offer came across my path. While the job in and of itself sounded good, nothing sounded as good to them as the words "stay in New York" and those words were not coming from my lips.

I had no choice but to tolerate their disappointment, their sadness and tuck it away in the dark place of my psyche where I kept the regret I heard in my friends' voices and my own guilt about leaving. I myself felt truly selfish and guilt-ridden about my decision to return to Philadelphia, but I justified it time and again by saying it was my turn to indulge myself and do what I wanted. That satisfied me for a while, but the guilt always returned.

That's where my parents' second wave of attack came into play. My mother sensed this internal struggle, these inner thoughts, as mothers always do. She saw that my attachment to home was growing weak with opportunity looming but that the battle was still being waged. Every look said it. Every criticism implied her knowledge and I noticed she was using it against me. When I was home alone, pondering my move, wondering whether it was the right decision, she'd call to "check on me," ask me about other job offers, tell me what other people – friends, colleagues, strangers – thought of my decision. Apparently, what the receptionist at her company thought was supposed to sway my decision.

But my mother was a devious brainwasher. She knew that what our neighbors thought of my move didn't matter, but she was trying to create the illusion that random people in society recognized how bad my decision was. I didn't fall for it, but it did hurt to hear it because in the random opinion polls of the mailman, check-out clerk and drycleaner, lay the truth about what my mother was feeling: that I was making a mistake. Worse yet, within her disappointment was hidden an even greater truth: that I knew she was right.

It is so easy to put off what's right, what comes naturally, because of fear. It is such a simple action to say no to your muse. I had never realized before how hard it was to make the decision to write and how easy it was to walk away. Or drink it away as I intended to do at my going away party.

Big Beer Night at The Scaffold Inn was certainly something to remember, or, more accurately, to forget. Every attendee was given a mug larger than your head from which to sip, although most of us guzzled. It was a direct flashback to college where I watched many a fraternity brother chug a pitcher of beer before my eyes. A friend once told me the secret was in opening your throat. I knew this advice was dodgy to say the least because he was the same person who told me his fraternity letters, SAE, stood for: "Sexual Assault Expected."

But that was college. I glanced over to check out the bathroom line and there didn't seem to be any sketchy frat boys around, so I made my way over saying "hi" to friends along the way. Marie and Sylvia were belly up at the bar and I thought of how far we had come from our days of high school glee club concerts, getting drunk on wine coolers and getting thrown out of stores like "Star Magic" for being "too rough with the kaleidoscopes." We'd run out the doors, a gaggle of giggles and end up at Ed Debevic's for chocolate milkshakes and french-fries. This happy hour was definitely not the first time we were standing legally at a bar, but sometimes it still struck me how far we had come as friends and adults.

The moment the three of us had said our good-byes and left for college, our paths had changed forever and I feared our friendship would also. Yet, over time it grew in depth and understanding, an incredible bond we often attributed to the fact that we didn't have sisters, making us take our friendships to one another and cling to them. We created our own definition of what sisterhood entailed, perhaps taking it more to heart because it was self-taught, self-made.

That's how we were when I entered college. I looked around my first few months of college and I saw a graveyard of failed friendships. I've never seen people so quick to shed their hometown friends as they donned sorority sweatshirts and fraternity boxer shorts. They couldn't wait to start over. It was as if they knew that college was the place where they never had to keep their promises of friendship. It was a transitional escape, an excuse to let a friendship go to the wayside and recreate your life, your persona. The "I miss you" and promise to write and call faded away into the backdrop of parties and classes and football games with the sorority sisters you swore you'd never be like.

But Marie, Sylvia and I hadn't fallen for that. I mean, I did fabricate a sorority so people would stop asking me where I was pledging, and Sylvia did join a very honorable co-ed food chemistry fraternity whose hazing involved Crisco and chicken giblets. Or so I made up. It was funnier to just imagine.

And that is how I saw it. We all had these separate, unique lives that somehow could never be independent of one another on a subtle emotional level. So, from the beginning of my college years, our college years, we refused to let one another's faces or voices fall into an irretrievable past. The events of that first semester only served to reinforce that commitment.

Amidst the parties and drunken fiascos during the first week of school, I learned quickly that preferring hard alcohol over beer could result in hospitalization; that the fourth floor bathroom of a frat house was always worth the walk; and that when someone says they are going to be sick, they're usually telling the truth, so step back. The world I was living in was surreal and in a week's time I was already drowning in the swirl of it. I probably would've gone under given more time if I hadn't received a sobering phone call: Marie's father had died suddenly of a heart attack back in New York.

After hearing the news, I made arrangements to be on the first train after class Friday night from Philadelphia to New York City and made it to the funeral home in the Bronx early Saturday morning. It was one of the most difficult days I had ever encountered in terms of digesting the shock while still trying to function normally: finding something to wear and getting myself to a funeral home in the Bronx being the two most important tasks. I settled on a traditional ensemble of black skirt and white blouse and was out the door. All I could think about on the drive there was that if it was this bad for me, I couldn't imagine what it was like for my best friend.

I have few memories of that entire day. It was a blur. I do remember stupidly not wearing my glasses and walking into the wrong salon at the funeral home. As I stood in the back wondering why the Irish Mr. Randolph had so many Asian friends and relatives, I was discreetly rescued by Marie's older brother who directed me to the proper place. At least my stupidity made him smile in the midst of all that had happened.

The only other memory I have is of finally walking into the right room and seeing Marie there and suddenly being thirteen again: the first day of school, knowing nothing about the world and our lives. I felt I had so little to offer as I sat down beside her. No moving words or sentiments came to me. I smiled and my eyes filled up with tears. As we hugged, I was almost sure she was comforting me more than I was soothing her.

It seemed that suddenly on this very day, in this funeral home, we were being thrown to the wolves. We were getting our first real taste of what else was in store. We thought college was it. We thought moving in and classes were the "real deal." But that was nothing. Here we were. Some people get that bitter taste earlier in life. We got it right on the cusp, the edge between the old world and the new. It was a glimpse into the rocky and unpredictable future of adulthood and, for me, a defining moment. It opened my eyes. When I went back to school, I saw everything differently. My surroundings had changed. Events were put into perspective. It was the worst thing that could've happened but somehow it helped me.

I wasn't with Marie again for at least a month after that day in the funeral home, but in letters and phone calls she appeared more than okay. As far as I knew, her grades were never dramatically poor, she never withdrew socially and she made friends there she would keep forever.

I never pretended to know what it was like – to begin a new life and have such an important part of my old one disappear. But I was blinded by the fierce presence of strength. I saw that strength could exist. I felt like Marie had taken it all and had never fallen apart. And somehow by knowing her, by being her friend, she made me stronger too.

I began to realize that in life those we keep close share their best and worst with us. Everyone touches us, even if ever so lightly, and those around us who are strong or brave or kind inspire those qualities in us. As friends, they often lift us up and make us better. My drunken party life in college may have shallowed me, may have led me in the wrong direction, but one sobering moment about the preciousness of life and family was enough to show me the people in life to hold onto and those to let go.

But there were people that we never have a choice about and those were the ones we wonder about and think about on drunken nights at happy hour bars. I quickly let the idea of Francis Laboure enter my mind. It seemed he had no place there in that part of my life, this time with my friends. He was an outsider and would probably stay that way. I was saddened by the thought of that, like somehow I wanted to make a place for him but I didn't know how and it was really too late. My sentimentality and/or many beers had gotten to me and my heart had never felt so full as I looked around.

Nor my bladder. Damn the bathroom line was slow. I finally made my way into the one-person restroom and took a long drunken look at myself in the dingy mirror. I tried to think of a way to turn back. Maybe I could stay. Did I really want to leave my friends? Did I really want to work in an advertising agency? Did I really want to leave the idea of this book to the wayside? Was this really what I wanted? I let my mind wander to the idea of staying but it was too far-gone. Then I thought about somehow making it all work, making it all fit together. Going to Philadelphia but continuing my writing project, still trying to find Francis and not giving up on my dream. I got a warm fuzziness inside but I wasn't sure if it was the Big Beer or the idea of maybe making things work despite my new situation.

Startled by a pounding on the door, I realized I had taken more than my fair share of time washing my hands. I opened the door and let the drunken girl rush in and shove me out as she slammed the door behind me. I slowly walked away, distracted by the dancing going on in the back of the bar and forgetting what I had been thinking. It was easier not to look back.

II. The End

Cristina T. Lopez

<u>Suspended Animation</u>

So, it was back to the City of Brotherly love. After I had graduated, after I had cried over every monument and building, after I had said good-bye to every Ivy Stone and every window that shed light on my daydreams, after I cried over this period of my life coming to an end and walked the campus walks trying to find meaning in it all, there it was again beyond the Benjamin Franklin Bridge. That city. A new beginning from the end. A new start to the finish.

My career at the ad agency, Potenta, began just as I knew it would. The atmosphere was fresh and different, vibrant with business. We were small but on the rise. I began at the very bottom and quickly moved up, something that happens when there is much to do and only a few people to do it. I did not mind. I had found my niche in the public relations field early on and began writing the more basic press releases for my clients.

I lived on my own, something I'd never be able to do in New York on my salary, at least not in the type of neighborhood I was living in. I had an apartment that was a stone's throw from Rittenhouse Square. I could walk to work and the gym too. I was going out every night, working hard every day and loving life. Sort of.

I felt this intense, insatiable gap in my life. There was work and there was going out but any semblance of deeper meaning was exhausted from my life after a ten or twelve-hour workday. Even if the energy was there, I was finding nothing to inspire me in the Philadelphia bar scene. Least of all love.

I cannot say that I was aloof and didn't try to find a boyfriend during my days and nights in Philadelphia. I was caught up in the conundrum of dating that the harder you look, the less you'll find. Every jackass from Pennsylvania, Delaware and New Jersey made his acquaintance with me and my romantic life became a parade of sad lonely hearts that saw me as someone to lean on.

My awful dating streak had last been punctuated by Chandler Bing, a very nice guy whose real name I can no longer even remember. We started talking in a bar because he had an uncanny resemblance to Matthew Perry's character on the hit-show, *Friends*. He was a cute guy whose personality was a dark void, i.e. non-existent. After one date, well-lit enough to reveal he looked NOTHING like Matthew Perry, he insisted on coming up to my apartment (lack of personality does not equal lack of persistence). It was early and I didn't mind the company so I let him hang out. Luckily, we both fell asleep fully dressed thanks to several glasses of wine at dinner. (In retrospect, I should have given him shots of tequila to liven him up.)

I awkwardly woke up to a very noticeable ticking and secretly cursed my cheap wristwatch for being so loud and waking me from my slumber. Oddly, when I held the timepiece to my ear, it was quietly ticking. My sudden movements woke up my bedmate. I asked if his watch was the culprit. He replied, "No, it's me." My confused look sparked the quick explanation of his artificial valve whose ticking often keeps others awake.

My mind raced to a scenario in which we would be so bored one night with so little to say that the ticking of his heart might overwhelm the conversation. In a desperate panic, I averted his bedroom eyes and imagined the horror of killing him in a moment of passion. I also dreaded feeling like Captain Hook with the ticking crocodile never far behind. So I guiltily cut our contact knowing my reasons were shallow but not wanting to pursue something with someone I did not really care for.

Upon finding out that things with Chandler Bing had taken a negative turn, my friends were quick to recommend I ask out the cute bartender, Harry, who worked at our local hangout, The Bistro. At first I resisted but the prospect of free food and beverage was overwhelming. So I gave in. But, alas, Harry the bartender had his own share of problems that I quickly became entangled in.

Aside from compulsive gambling, revealed on our first date to Atlantic City where he lost all his money and part of my own, Harry suffered from severe alcoholism. He often forgot our "dates" (time spent in a bar with him getting bombed and me making polite conversation with strangers), our conversations and, I suspected, my name. There was a lot of "Hey, baby" and "Hi, Sweetie" where my name should've been inserted. Harry didn't seem to know much about me at all and I believed he was afraid to ask for fear we had already discussed it. He'd call me on the phone several times in one night forcing me to repeat the same conversation with him again and again, back to back.

I should have given up sooner but the drinks at The Bistro were not cheap and I liked Harry's discount. Plus, he was amusing to talk about with my friends. Best of all, I did not have to do anything physical with him to keep him interested. The most comical aspect of our "relationship" (although I doubt it qualified as such) was Harry's habit of showing up at my apartment drunk, watching TV with me, then undressing into his T-shirt and boxers and passing out. The next morning, he'd awake with a proud smile on his face believing he had conquered me with his sexual prowess. I could have, and should have, stopped this the moment I realized what Harry had assumed about us, but my friends and I were reaping the substantial benefits of my escapade with unlimited food and drink at the Bistro for "Harry's Girl."

After several weeks of his antics, I couldn't stand it any longer. I told Harry to call me when he was sober. I guess he kept "forgetting" because he never did. One night, I refused to let him come inside when he was drunk and I reasserted that he should call me the next day when he was sober. That must've triggered something when he awoke the next day NOT in my apartment. I guess he sensed something bad had happened but, because he couldn't remember exactly what, he continued to shower me and my friends with gratis treats. This continued until he was eventually fired for not showing up to work.

I forced myself to be firm and not give in to the temptation of dating for the sake of having a date. I tapered off my attempts to be part of the singles scene and decided it was more fun to be a witness. It seemed nicer from the outside, watching all of my friends go to fancy restaurants, clubs and cigar bars; cook romantic dinners for their dates and enjoy their company on moonlit walks. But for me, I knew better.

The only things I extracted from the dating scene were fake, rotten or shallow. Perhaps it was me. I don't think I was ready for what I was getting myself into. I seemed to attract the wrong guys and, when I attracted the right guys, the times being so few and far between, there was this elaborate game that my friends and coworkers tried to make me play. With all the "call him after three days" and "you didn't tell him you wanted to see him, did you?" I was inevitably left completely clueless as to what men wanted, but sure it wasn't someone like me. I gave up on all of it certain of only one thing: dating was not worth it for all the headaches it caused.

I decided to lay low and enjoy the better things in life. I had a good job and a great place to live. So I focused myself on that.

<u>Condemnation</u>

If it is true that physical elements in our lives, the brick and mortar that surround us, can reflect our mental state, then what happened to my building in Philadelphia was a definite signal that something was wrong. I moved into the building happily with a rent that was so cheap, it was almost too good to be true. Interesting thought.

When the cold weather began, my parents warned me to bundle up, telling me horror stories from when they lived in an apartment and had no heat. They told me how often people living in rented apartments have issues with heat, usually never having enough. I assured them I had plenty of heat. I did. As the winter kicked in, I had more than enough heat. Too much almost, but I would never complain because I constantly was reminded by my parents how lucky I was to have any at all.

As it got colder outside, it only grew warmer inside my apartment. I had my four windows open at all times, despite the danger of robbery. I came home and immediately undressed, opened the back door and turned my fan on. I would wake up each morning in a sweat, take a cold shower and then bundle up to go to a freezing cold office in comparison. But I was lucky. At least I had heat!

I would cook dinner for the poor soul I was dating at the time, one of the ones I was trying to play this ridiculous dating game with and losing very badly. I was lucky enough to get him over for dinner one night. The best advantage of uncontrollable heat was that before the main course was served, he was already sitting in his boxers at the table. It was perfect. Perhaps I could win this game after all.

But my thirst was unquenchable. I was positive I was losing weight when I woke up each morning in a pool of sweat. But at least I had heat!

Then, I reached the breaking point. I woke up one morning hotter than ever and when I went to the bathroom to splash cold water on my face, I burned my thighs on the bathroom sink. The porcelain was hot. My toiletries had all melted. My toothpaste was liquid. I had to squat over the toilet for fear of burning my backside. I used oven mitts to turn on the shower. This wasn't heat. This was hell!

I exited my apartment as soon as possible and called the management company who assured me this would be looked into. They discovered that the thermostat had no gauge controlling the heat. Therefore, the heat would go on, but there was no control telling it to turn off. When I told my parents, they told me they suspected something was wrong. No one in a rented apartment had that much heat. It was impossible.

A few weeks later, I realized how the heating issue had happened. The real-estate company who managed the building was selling it and it had finally been bought so maintenance was really the responsibility of the new owners. So things were only fixed on a need basis. I received a letter stating that the sale was complete and a new company was taking over as of February 1st. I was relieved.

Work began. Painting was done. Light fixtures were being...fixed. It was great. I went to do laundry one day and found a huge ditch in the basement exposing a leaking pipe. I was scared that there was no notice or sign stating not to go in the basement, but at least they were fixing it. I stepped around it and did my laundry.

A few days later, I came home and had difficulty opening my door. It was jammed. I finally pushed it open and exploded into my apartment. When I turned around to close the door, I discovered that the dead bolt was hitting itself. It was as if the door had shifted and I could no longer close it. I put the chain on, left the door hanging open and called the management. They would send a man the next day to take care of my problem. I slept that night with my door partially open.

The next day I left for work while the man attempted to see what was wrong with my door. I told him that the closet along the same wall had a similar problem: I had trouble opening it and now I couldn't close it. He said he'd look into it. I went to work.

When I came home that night, I found several men standing in my hallway with jackets that said "L&I." I had no idea who they were. I went into my apartment. The man had moved the lock up the door so that it would now fit. Interesting solution. I checked my messages and read my mail. Then came the knock at the door.

In my doorway, a middle-aged woman who identified herself as a social worker greeted me. She was there to tell me my options. I had no idea what she was talking about. She thought I had been briefed. She apologized and then told me that the City of Philadelphia's Licensing and Inspection department had condemned my building. Apparently, the shifting of the building's foundation caused by unlicensed construction work had scared a tenant into calling the city because his floorboards had curled up. I realized that the trouble with my doors was from the building now leaning to one side. The city had deemed my apartment unsafe and I had to leave.

I stayed with a friend since my "option" consisted of going to a homeless shelter. The real estate company provided me with nothing.

The building was officially condemned a week later, which I discovered while I was home in New York for St. Patrick's Day. My friends insisted this was a sign to move back to New York, but I refused to give in. I saw moving home as defeat. I wanted to prove that I could live on my own and take care of my own problems without having to turn myself over to the care of my parents.

I returned to Philadelphia and found a new apartment, but never shook the feeling that my building being condemned was not a good indicator of the state of my life. The foundation of my home was warping and crumbling and I had no idea. I hadn't noticed. What did that say about my life?

Fading Out

When I finally resurfaced in a new apartment, I thought my life in Philadelphia might start to turn around. My friends and I were still having good times out and about and although work was beginning to feel stifling, it seemed to be going well. My responsibilities increased but so did my working late nights and weekends. When I wasn't working on the weekends, I found myself traveling home to New York to lift up my spirits. I felt like I had not found a niche in one life so I was riding between both. Eventually, I sensed I was entering a state of depression. I was lonely and I still felt this gnawing gap within me. Nothing I was doing in my current life was taking away that feeling. I turned again to writing.

Having abandoned the search, I had nothing to write about Francis. So I tried other types of creative outlets. I could not bring myself to scrawl out a poem or a short story. I was too undisciplined for that. Instead I started writing letters. I resurrected the tradition of writing weekly to my old friend, Leia, even though we hadn't spoken in years.

But, I felt trapped. I felt I had something to say and no one to direct my words to. She seemed like a good place to start.

Leia had always been someone I could relate to in a letter, someone who would read and appreciate my thoughts. I never mailed those rants I wrote to her about the senseless dirt and violence all around me. The bitterness in my tone was evident and I never wanted to mail something like that to another person, let alone someone I hadn't seen or heard from in years. When I reread my words, it seemed I was aching for something greater than myself and greater than my life to inspire me. But there was nothing there. I was calling out in an empty chamber, my words reached out into nothingness, echoing there sadly with no reply:

> "If I even knew where to begin, I would start there, but I cannot. My mind swims even though it's burning up in flames. It's racing but my thoughts go nowhere. And 'one of those days' is a trite, irrelevant phrase for how my time is really spent.
>
> "I'm sitting in the Peter Pan bus station in Philadelphia on the Friday before Labor Day Weekend trying to get out of one city only to go to another: New York. I've had quite a day, punctuated only by a cab driver who couldn't break a

twenty or get me to the bus on time, a bus driver who for once in his life felt compelled to leave three minutes early instead of late, and a woman at the ticket window whose ignorance and slow pace were excelled only by her foul breath that penetrated the air holes of the bulletproof glass.

"And if you thought because I was able to sit with headphones over my ears drowning out the screams of a four year old who wants to do as he pleases, I'm tuned out, you're wrong. I'm not. If you think I should be used to life in the city just because I've lived in or near one since I was born, you're wrong. And anyone who is, is not only desensitized but also victimized by whomever or whatever convinced them this is normal. It's not.

"Mothers shouldn't hit their children in public while those very same children scream out for them. Homeless men shouldn't flirt with me and overweight women shouldn't wear tight Lycra shorts and half shirts while I'm trying to eat a ham sandwich.

"Just because it happens, doesn't make it right. It makes it reality. It makes it available to my reality, but it doesn't make sense at all, which is what this pen is attempting to do with it. I'm trying to make this surrealism real, this strangeness familiar in the context of my bad day. But it's not familiar. Every time I see ugly odd images of society's discontent, it's like I see it for the first time again. All I can hope is that because it remains so foreign to my senses, those same senses will immediately recognize normalcy. But it's been so long since I've seen normalcy, I'm not sure if it exists anymore.

"I used to think normalcy was childhood, but how can that be? Childhood was a time when anything made sense and fantasy and reality could not be distinguished from one another. As a child, the bizarre rainbow ponies and plastic figures of skinny, large-breasted women with great clothing living in dollhouses was normal. Puppets singing tub songs and animated cat people from outer space were just as much a part of reality as mom and dad.

"I'm all grown up now. Childhood is over. The lines between the classroom, where history is reality, and the playground, where fantasy is reality, are still blurred. Now my dreams are a conscious escape instead of a subconscious relapse. The starkest realities seem to be a dream: the heavyset prostitute selling her used vagina to odd, lonely men who stare vacantly into its depth; the homeless man, riddled with fungus, eating moldy scraps; or the young man who scratches his scalp and eats what remains beneath his fingernails. In this dream, the beginning is its end and the end never begins. I'm in a state of mind so incoherent I cannot say I know where to begin and, even if I did, I wouldn't start because to dig so deep is almost always the wrong direction to take. I know that if I took that journey you'd inevitably have to come with me and I don't have the heart to take you there."

Something had to change.

Fading In

Eventually, the Bistro faded into a remote past and other local watering holes demanded our time like Copa Too!, a small, cozy margarita bar. Pouring over a large strawberry margarita and commiserating about work and the lousy dating scene, the story of Francis slowly came to light. I told my friends about my attempt to find Francis Laboure and my idea to write a book about the experience. For a moment, I felt like my old self: confident and talented. There was so much there, bottled up inside, waiting for the moment to burst forth and shine. But, when the questions about the current state of the manuscript came up, all those good feelings collapsed and I was almost too ashamed to tell the truth: that I had abandoned the book to work for Potenta and that I had never actually found the long-lost Francis.

It was within that discussion, embedded with undertones of dissatisfaction with my life, that I realized my time had come to take leave of Potenta. Two years had passed and I was still looking for something, needed something and it was just not emerging from my life in Philadelphia. There were too many voices calling me back to New York. My brother had recently announced that he and my sister-in-law were having a baby. Marie and her boyfriend, Sam, were just engaged. My parents were pining for their "little baby." I had conquered the dating scene, or it had conquered me.

Most of all, I missed being creative. No matter how lofty my ideas were about being able to put my writing aside and work full time, it was not a fulfilling life for me. I thought I could get away with not being creative, not focusing on what little talent existed in me, but the idea of Francis was a quiet reminder of a part of me I was ignoring that wanted to come alive. It became obvious to me that it was time to return home to face a challenge and share in all the new happenings in the lives of those I loved.

Before I knew it, I was riding in the front seat of my father's steel-gray Chevy Astrovan filled with my belongings. We drove on the New Jersey Turnpike and I tried to fight nausea with sleep, but really was sitting with my eyes closed thinking about my writing and my life.

Despite my desire to return home, I found it difficult to say good-bye to Philadelphia. The friends that I had made there felt so close to me even though I knew that we were about to scatter. But they were proof that I had made a place for myself in the City of Brotherly Love, albeit one more sisterly than anything else.

Yet, my friends alone were proof that my life in Philadelphia was not ever permanent. They were a lot like me: transients passing through. After I announced my move, I found many of them also leaving for greener pastures. Many of us had existed there on a temporary basis and although I could not see it at the time, we were shadowed always by a desire to be something better, to accomplish more. I knew that I'd never be able to stay focused and push forward in the way it would take to get ahead in the industry. I knew that eventually I'd have to face the fact that I needed more to feel fulfilled.

My experience during the final months in Philadelphia, the strange dating encounters, my apartment being condemned, all solidified why I was moving and what I wanted to accomplish. I realized my heart and mind were so full of stories and those ideas were not emerging in press releases or articles on vinyl flooring. For the first time in my life, I was making the conscious decision to put my writing first when I'd spent so long putting it last, if not hiding it from the world. I felt committed to this new identity as a writer and for some reason that notion made moving back in with my parents without a job prospect felt like some type of triumph because I was going to write no matter what.

Perhaps it was the act of starting over that invigorated me. I saw it more as a new beginning than a return to New York with my tail between my legs. Perhaps, someone else would have seen her return to her parents' house jobless, apartmentless and close to penniless as being a failure but I felt that it was a humbling fresh start. I had new challenges ahead that I had yet to tap into. I felt unstoppable. I finally felt like I was coming home.

I decided to find a job after the summer to "accommodate my writing" and I would live at home to save money. I'd rekindle the old, important friendships I'd been missing out on and say good-bye to

Philadelphia, for real this time. I was looking forward to spending a few months bonding with my newborn nephew.

It was surprising to me that I had always envisioned writing as an activity that takes the author on journeys far away from my family and friends. Movies and television had always depicted the search for a long-lost friend as being an event that takes the individual to the ends of the earth just to find out whatever became of them. Yet, my search was the driving force bringing me home.

I realized then that at the moment when the vision seemed most lost and most confused, it is best to return to the beginning and start again. I felt lucid, clean, fresh and lucky. I was starting over and there was so much good in my life to write about.

Cristina T. Lopez

III. The Beginning Again

Cristina T. Lopez

<u>The Wee Kevin</u>

I've said it once and I'll say it again: the best form of birth control for a single, twenty-something female is to spend ten hours a day with a three-month-old infant.

I returned to New York and decided to accept my brother's offer to nanny for my nephew until they could figure out a long-term plan for that baby boy and I could secure a job for myself that would allow me to find Francis.

It was quite an atypical summer from the experiences my friends were having in their own jobs. I would wake up in the morning on my brother's sofa bed, sit up and rub my eyes. Immediately I was handed a smiling, laughing cherub with cheeks still ruddy from breast feeding for 45 minutes, still warm from cuddling close to his mom as he nursed. That ruddiness, laughter and smiling slowly dissipated over the course of each morning as I struggled to determine what made him winge and cry; was it hunger, sleepiness, gas, a dirty diaper or just lack of attention?

121

My nephew would cry and I would check his diaper, hold him, feed him and still the lower lip would tremble and he'd look at me like his jailer and torturer. There was horror and betrayal in his eyes as they begged the question: "What have you done with my mother?" Some days I could cheer him. But, sometimes, I just could not fix it. On more difficult days, he'd cry himself to sleep, only a short-term relief from which he'd usually awaken with the cause of distress still present.

Despite thoughts and conjectures that this situation would improve over time, it only became more complicated as he grew. A month into nannying, I was trying to win over the affections of an old college flame, James. James would call me during the day to talk about work and catch up on our lives, his obviously much different than mine at that time. I'd be wrestling with Kevin who was crying in frustration as he tried to turn himself over but could not release his one arm.

Or, James would call just as I was getting the baby down for a nap. I would pretend it wasn't a big deal because he was a nice guy and, after my terrible track record in Philadelphia, I very much wanted him to like me. But it seemed our lives were not synchronizing. What young guy wanted to hear about my nephew's latest antics of kicking and twisting himself in his highchair until he sank down, belted in, contorted and uncomfortable as he drooled and moaned from the dreadful pain of new teeth emerging? I called the baby my "Wounded Soldier" because of the long, painful moans that would emerge from his carriage as we walked down the aisles of the drug store. James didn't find this very amusing. These just were not topics that seemed of interested to him. I knew I was putting our relationship to the test. He wanted my full attention and I felt distracted.

I was pre-experiencing motherhood and learning things I never thought I would, such as the frustrations of not being able to go to the bathroom without song and dance and then either leaving the baby strapped in his high chair for safety or bringing him in his low seat into the bathroom with me, a humiliating experience for both of us. Then there was the embarrassment of going on a dinner date smelling of breast milk.

I soon faced moments of frustration where, after four hours of his crying, I would begin to cry too. The baby would stop his crying to stare at me like I was an alien, not his aunt or nanny. Suddenly, I would realize that I was the one acting like a baby and began to laugh. But this only startled the baby who then would begin to cry all over again. Then the phone would ring and I'd try to explain this all to James with no success. He wanted my full attention and focus and I was being stretched thin to provide it.

I knew I was experiencing something life-changing when in the midst of this pathetic and seemingly endless cycle of changing dirty diapers (so intensely soiled that they force the inevitable question: "Has someone been feeding the baby raw spinach?"), wiping the drool from his chin or blocking the stream of urine aimed at my new blouse while I changed him, Kevin would laugh. He would look up and smile at me, chuckling, as if to say, "This is funny, don't you think?" I would then realize that these so-called "offensive" acts — the smelly farts, the cheesy vomit – were just evidence of pure innocence. What would normally be a declaration of war from another adult was merely a new and necessary experience for this baby, this boy, this little man, who was growing and changing everyday, who learned to hug as he learned to hold, who learned to kiss as he learned to eat. For every tear there was a laugh twice as precious.

I got angry with myself for losing patience because, for me, this was short term. At the end of the summer, when work called again, I would say my good-byes and retire my nanny overalls. Then I would have to rise each day to face a shower and a commute, not a baby. But, I would remember that face, that trusting soul who just wanted to eat and sleep and play and poop in peace. I hated myself for my frustrations and lack of insight into what he was: an angel born to remind me how precious life is. From a glass of milk to a walk in the park, the little things are a foundation for all the great ones. He was a great one at six months when I stopped being his nanny and that potential for greatness increased exponentially every day, to this day. It would grow into his childhood, into his manhood and all I could hope for was that my time with him was as strong an influence on him as he'd been on me.

I wondered about influence and I realized that his beauty, innocence, and fresh face contained the sparks of what my own childhood was to me. What those faces showed to me, what they told me about the world; how they softened my heart. Children inspire us because they bring our hearts back to when we were children; they allow us to rediscover a better time. Spending this time with my nephew was a brief glimpse of parenthood and a short lesson of what I was looking for in my own life.

I realized that in my work and in my personal, romantic relationships I was getting away from the things that I cared about, surrounding myself with people who didn't always inspire me to be better or follow my dreams and that was deteriorating my spirit. I didn't want to just go through the motions, I wanted to live a life and work toward a dream I cared about. Moving to New York and starting over was an important first step but I knew I had to break off the relationships that didn't have meaning and seek out those that did. So I did just that.

After that summer, I said concluded my stint as my nephew's nanny, which he took quite gracefully happy to have his mom home full-time, and said good-bye to James, who, unfortunately, did not take our break-up as well. But, I knew I was doing the right thing and I was ready for action.

My next step was to obtain a job that would enable me to continue my search for Francis Laboure. Having experienced being a nanny, I suddenly realized what it was to have influence on those around me. I wanted to answer the question, "What impact do I have on the world? On the people in my life? To what extent do I change the world by what I do and say?" It was easy to look at my own family and see how it had changed with the baby's birth. But, what difference had I made as a nanny? What if a stranger had cared for Kevin for those three months? How different would he be? How different would I be? The possibilities were endless. My possibilities were endless.

I had abandoned the search for Francis before moving to Philadelphia because I had felt that the search was innately selfish and that I should not overturn this stone without better reason than my own curiosity. But with this fresh start so clear to me I realized that even though the reason why I was looking for Francis had not changed, I had. My determination to find him seemed to shift in its driving force. "Where is Francis Laboure?" remained the question but the surrounding issues changed as what was significant to me shifted into insignificance and new priorities emerged.

I started looking for Francis because I thought I wanted to find him and write about the process. But, I realized that I wanted to write and Francis was letting me. Despite this self-focused reasoning, I felt that what I was doing was important. I was trying to uncover the mystery of his memory and uncover the role, however small, I had in his life. This process had been a driving force in my work and I had to accept that. I felt obligated to it. I wanted to continue.

I no longer needed to find Francis Laboure. But the truth was that I still wanted to.

Conversations with the Dead

It may seem odd to address death following such praise and awe of my nephew's new life, but with his birth I found myself paying attention to the very distinct patterns of life that touch us all. At every turn, with every gesture, I saw someone else emerge in him: my father's smirk, my mother's mischievousness, my brother's looks, my own anal retentiveness. I saw all of us in him.

I looked at my family and I could not help but think of where we were all going. What would happen to the many phases of our family's generations? One night at a family dinner, my parents, siblings and I discussed the different lives my parents would have led if they had never left Cuba, if they had never both come to New York and met. My mother was certain that whether or not she had left Cuba, she would have met and married my father and we would have all been born just the same. I disagreed. I think in Cuba, her life would have been different and her influences would have been different. Even if she had met my father and my brothers and I were born, our lives would have been different. Our paths completely changed. My nephew, with an Irish-American mother, could not have been born.

The conversation sparked the already existing question in my mind of what time and timing meant to families. So much was fate and chance and the right people meeting in the right places. Even within a family, time meant everything. Over years, so much could change. Two who were close could suddenly drift away. Our elders passed on as new children were born. Our lives had changed when my grandfather died and so much more when my nephew was born.

The endless emotional tide of those drifting in and out of our lives is a notion that fascinates me. I constantly piece together all these faces and names that I have encountered throughout my life. These are individuals who, while leading me into new friendships, slowly fade into the backdrop. My mind wanders over the many friends of friends who I perhaps felt close to one summer at a shore house but then eventually lost touch with; or someone's parents I met one winter on a ski trip and then never saw again. I remember them, perhaps I laughed with them or shared something special, a moment. Do they remember me? Is the memory important? Do I ever have a significant impact on the people whose lives I briefly touched?

I couldn't put my finger on what I was doing mentally but I finally called it "having conversations with the dead" because I could not let go the idea of influence. It seemed that the things and people that had often influenced my life, had such hold on my memories, were those that were long gone from this world, or at least my world.

I was defining the dead as not only those who pass away and physically die, but those no longer with us, those dead to us. People die in our lives all the time and it does not involve wakes and funerals. People die when we no longer see them, speak to them, know them or watch them grow. The dead are not the unknown but the known no longer, for one cannot be dead unless they were once alive to us.

Sometimes the dead are resurrected. Sometimes we recall the dead and keep them alive in our memories. I was finding that losing touch with people in my life was just as traumatic and sad as losing someone in true physical death. But it was a different type of sadness: one slowly emerging and worsening over time with the effects felt more each day. To me, this was unlike traditional death whose effect faded and grew tolerable after the initial blow. For those we lose to distance and change alone, the extra burden was the guilt of knowing they are out there somewhere but never having the heart to reconnect with them, letting too much time go by until their figural death is literal and reconciliation too late. These are the childhood friends or college buddies whom we never called after winter break and the more time went by, the more it seemed too late.

In remembering the "dead" souls in my life: school friends, pen pals or ex-boyfriends no longer in my space, there was deep emotion, often disdain or memories of arguments and wrongdoing. Sometimes we lose touch with others for significant reasons such as disloyalty or anger. Their loss is reaffirmed by the memories of when they were a part of our lives and the realization of the necessity in letting them go.

But beyond the fights and heartaches that spoke to me so clearly, there were memories that lacked clarity. There were voices from my past whose absence I could not quite make out. There was no tone, no content, and no indication as to whether it was right or wrong to say good-bye. That curiosity ate away at my insides with utterances of "What if what if what if???" One of those people was Francis Laboure.

Francis was a child I knew when I was six years old. A child who had a party to celebrate his birthday and I was the only guest who attended. He was a child who cried the whole afternoon, even as my mom picked me up to take me home. He was a boy whom I never saw again after that day, whom I never spoke about with my classmates after he left, who I let slip away into a graveyard of memories. Francis lay among the dead in my mind, a boy whose beacon was present but silent, making it all the more mysterious, all the more alluring, but all the more frightening as well. My determination was stronger than ever to find him but the outcome was more unclear and elusive than ever before.

Cristina T. Lopez

My plan was in action: I had obtained my optimal 9 to 5 job in order to continue writing this book. It wasn't easy to convince headhunters to place a former Account Executive as a Typist but I managed to convince them I would be satisfied in this line of work if it could afford me the opportunity to write my book. Obtaining a position in database entry for an auction house was an exciting conquest, not for the job itself but for its impact on my life. The job forced me to fight for this book, fight to give it a place and meaning while allowing it to flourish. There would be no more work to take home or nightmares about deadlines and clients.

I was ready to embark on the journey of finding Francis. I wanted to take my time in finding him, take time to discover my true goals before I got too involved in the outcome, take time to think out, write out and investigate the writing world.

My first step was to make contact with other writers and agents. It seemed that there was a shared excitement induced by the search. Their reactions injected me with new enthusiasm and the belief that I was onto something: that my story of a search for one man was really a story about conquering the death sentence we often unintentionally pass on those who enter and exit our lives. My story, albeit small, was perhaps bigger in the context of the universe that is our lives.

Sitting in the Shadow of a Puppy

My search for Francis and the writing process involved was certainly fulfilling when I wasn't overwhelmed with work. How did that happen? I took my new job with every intention of committing myself to my writing. But then it began. That undying need to do a good job, impress people, make SOME type of progress and to never leave a job half-done at the end of the day. I was certainly improving my typing skills but I was unable to use them for what I wanted: to write my book.

Being employed in an internationally prominent auction house was something to be proud of. Taking a job as a typist in order to be better focused on my writing was certainly commendable. But I didn't feel proud. I didn't feel accomplished. I was caught up in typos and timesheets instead of chapters and edits. I was lacking focus and dedication to the project. I did finally get into my writing but it took ten months after I began working full-time again for that to happen. And, even when I did begin, I was not producing enough to characterize myself as an "author." Luckily, my poetry had begun to flourish inside short staccato lines that were sharp and bitter, a reflection of how I felt.

So, I kept focused on Francis though the pace was slow. I was diverted. Summertime was approaching. The beach was calling. Outdoor happy hours. Monday movie night at Bryant Park. But also, even more, the world I had injected myself into had become a fascinating sideshow.

I found the auction world to be a beautiful shell enclosing a dark place of greed. I had left advertising because of its profit-obsessed nature and walked into a world where art equaled only a dollar value. I slowly realized that the beauty I had always associated with art was lost to high/low auction estimates or the taboo "NSV" signifying No Sale Value. God forbid.

At first I thought it was just my perspective as a typist. I was at the bottom looking up. I received an e-mail saying a company was like a tree full of monkeys: those who look down only see smiling faces, those who look up only see assholes. Maybe I was jealous. Maybe I missed the feelings of authority and accomplishment that came from working hard and being recognized for achievements. I was in a position that required minimal effort and, because of that, there was no glory. I stuck to my rationale and my drive that I was making this sacrifice for my career. But my eyes could not help noticing what was happening around me.

Not even the employees with "real" jobs seemed to be having fun. Their jobs were endless drudgery for them just like mine was for me. With little rewards, low salaries, long hours and for what? Works of art whose location is inevitably "Basement" or "Storage."

It would've made me cry if I had really cared. I had my book to love. I didn't need to love this place. But soon, I was so caught up in the hurricane of this appraisal and that affidavit that even the book was put away and I was just the typist. Francis was again just a distant fragment of who I was. He was a manuscript in a drawer that I was waiting for a slow day to work on. My focus was elsewhere.

At least I had a strong company to stand behind, I'd say to myself: a solid foundation, a good corporation to work for. And then that too crumbled. The very core of the auction business opened itself to reveal decaying within: price-fixing. Whether or not allegations were true, it was just one more image shattered. When you scraped the paint away, not even honesty lay beneath. I didn't find many surprised by it. Soon, even I became jaded to the discoveries. But I missed beauty. I missed looking at art and seeing art, not auctions and estimates and appraisals.

So, I would try to remind myself of beauty by going out at lunch and sitting in Rockefeller Center on a sunny day in the shadow of *Puppy*, a monumental flowering sculpture shaped like a dog. Amazing in its size (about two to three stories), overwhelming in its stature and endearing in its cuteness, I looked at this gargantuan piece and its list of sponsors and thought, "At least my company was a part of this. At least they helped bring this beauty to the public. Perhaps the beauty of art is not completely lost to it."

But, as I checked over the list of sponsors featured prominently on the flowing banner, I saw my company's name had been omitted. The prominent, international auction house had not helped bring it here. It had nothing to do with this sculpture so lovely that the birds rested their eggs inside and sang to it.

No, our corporation was not part of this beauty. But I still was. I could still sit in the midst of something beautiful and enjoy it. I could still appreciate the devastating grace of art, of nature in art, of human nature, of the souls drifting by me in the plaza. I could recognize the beauty that transcends value; still know the value that is inner beauty. I wanted to drift away from Rockefeller Plaza, a universe of the "beautiful" people, and the home of the gigantic white smile of Katie Couric on the side of the NBC Studio. It seemed the monumental posture of *Puppy* might not be enough to protect me. I longed to vanish into Central Park instead of going back inside my office.

But, instead, I sat within the shadow of *Puppy* watching a solitary butterfly make its way inside an ear and wrote all this down. I would keep writing it down. I had to keep telling my story because it was what kept me going.

Resurrecting All Saints

I re-read the events taking place when I began my search for Francis Laboure and I realized that, while I did face several obstacles, the bottom line was I hadn't succeeded because I hadn't tried hard enough. I kept letting work stand in my way. I also had moved to Philadelphia that summer after college graduation and never called back P.S. 66 in the fall to see if Francis had been enrolled there and where he may have gone after. I had dropped the reigns and abandoned the dedication with which I had started.

My move to New York came from a need to begin again, this time with less uncertainty and hesitation, more resolve and courage. A year later, I felt as if I had outgrown the fear and trepidation surrounding my first visit to my grammar school. I had regained my perspective and a newfound dedication to this project. This time I would not take "no" for an answer.

Time had also given me another advantage: forgetfulness. I was hoping that after several years of being away, my first embarrassing, almost humiliating visit would be forgotten. I was right.

My timing and strategy when calling back All Saints was a lot smarter the second time around. I called just as the school day had ended: late enough that the day's craziness was out the door but not late enough that the illegality of my request would be considered. The immediate familiarity of the receptionist's nasty tone made me twinge. I simply and strongly stated my request: I needed assistance in locating a former classmate. I was put on hold as she called over the principal.

I mentally patted myself on the back for not going over there in person. A few years in the workforce had taught me some valuable lessons on first impressions that I had not yet known my first time around. I had actually thought that getting all dressed up in a suit and heels and ringing the doorbell gave me some type of advantage with the old biddies. No way. Two years of public relations taught me that I was much more important over the phone. There is a certain power in the fax, the conference call and e-mail: self-aggrandizing was necessary, possible and worked best when no one could see you.

After repeating my request to the principal, I was put on hold so she could consider it. Would she have to dig through endless cobweb-mangled files to find his name? Would she put me off again with assumptions of what school Francis had *possibly* gone to? Not even three minutes passed when she was back on the phone.

"Hello?"

"Yes, I'm still here."

"Ms. Lopez?"

"Yes?"

"Francis Laboure left All Saints in the spring of 1982 and transferred to P.S. 66 in Hollis."

"Really?" I blurted out, kicking myself for saying that.

"Yes, really," she replied, as if to say "No, I'm lying to you. I'm a big fat nun and I'm lying to you because I get a kick out of doing it."

"Thank you so much!"

"You're welcome."

Click.

I was overjoyed! A real lead! It wasn't much but it added to my newfound confidence. I had real information from a valid and quotable source. I was on my way.

I immediately called information and obtained the number for P.S. 66. I wanted to do this right away but I hesitated: bullying a nun into divulging information was one thing. But public school was another story. Public. The city. I almost felt like somehow the mayor could get involved. It was a ridiculous notion but I was scared as I dialed the number. An administrative person answered and once again I explained my request. She said a request like that would have to be made in writing. Already the bureaucratic wheels were turning. I agreed to send off a letter, obtained the principal's information and hung up the phone.

Click.

I drafted my letter that same day. Yes, my job was really that slow.

9 November 1999

James Lemelson
Principal
Public School 66
91-37 333rd Street
Hollis, NY 11428

Dear Mr. Lemelson,

Per my telephone call to your office, I am sending this letter of introduction to you in the hopes that you will be able to assist my small, yet urgent, request.

I attended All Saints Elementary School from September of 1979 (Pre-school) through June of 1985 when I transferred to Saint Anthony of Padua School. I graduated from Saint Anthony's in June of 1989.

During my few years at All Saints, I became close to a young man named Francis Laboure who, after a small incident in 1982, transferred from All Saints to your school, P.S. 66, to begin second grade.

I am writing this letter because I would like to contact Francis but am having difficulty locating him. I do not want to see his records. I would just like to know what school he attended after leaving P.S. 66. I don't believe that information is confidential. It is a small endeavor that is very meaningful to me.

I would prefer, as I think you would as well, to discuss this matter in person, or, if need be, via telephone. I will call you Monday of next week to set up an appointment with you. But in the meantime, please feel free to contact me at my home or office at the numbers enclosed.

Even if you have read this letter and are unable to assist me, I would still like to speak to you to perhaps obtain your assistance and/or recommendations on other ways I might be able to locate my friend.

Thank you in advance for your time.

Sincerely,

Cristina T. Lopez

With that, I waited. I knew he'd never call but it gave me a valid

excuse to call back and ask again. Having a letter on file made a big

difference. As a writer, I liked this approach. In two weeks, I called back.

Understandably, Principal Lemelson did not get on the phone. It was a

lot safer to use his secretary as the intermediary, in case, say, I ever published a book and told the story about how a public school principal opened a former student's files at the request of a stranger.

"What's the call in reference to, Miss?"

"A letter I had sent to Principal Lemelson regarding a former classmate."

"Did you attend P.S. 66?"

"No."

"Please hold."

Should I have lied? They could easily verify if it was true and then I would've lost my credibility. No, the truth was better. I waited for what seemed like a long while. It was probably about two minutes.

"Hello."

"Yes."

"Why are you trying to locate this person?"

"Personal reasons. He was a friend."

My mind raced with the judgment of whether or not the statement was true. Verdict: true enough. Proceed.

"Hold on."

I waited again.

"Hello."

"Yes."

"Ms. Lopez, we cannot tell you what school Francis Laboure transferred to."

"I see."

"However, we can tell you that upon his departure from P.S. 66, Francis's records were sent on to Saugerties, New York."

"Saugerties?"

"Yes."

"How do you spell that?"

"S-A-U-G-E-R-T-I-E-S."

"And that's all the information you have?"

"To give you? Yes. That is where his records were last sent."

"Well, okay. Thank you."

Click.

I sat at my desk for ten minutes suppressing the desire to vomit. I then took a deep breath, took my mouse in hand and moved it quickly once to "wake up" my sleeping monitor. I clicked opened the Internet icon and entered a web address I had seen pop up on my TV after an episode of *The Jerry Springer Show* [I know what you are thinking. Shut up. I was sick at home.]: www.searchinusa.com.

Is this what I had been reduced to? I clicked the small ⊠ button and closed the connection. There had to be a better, more eloquent way to locate Francis. One that did his memory justice. One that didn't make my search, my book, my work into an episode of *The Ricki Lake Show*. One that was poetic and beautiful, like Fate.

But we had already forced Fate's hand. What would it hurt to push it a little bit more?

Search Results

It was a typical post-holiday morning at work: the person in front of me let the security door slam in my face, my boss ignored my good morning and all my projects were marked "Urgent ASAP." So, I did what I always did when things were urgent and I was cranky: I went to the bathroom to think.

The trick is to always put one stall between you and the other person in the bathroom if at all possible. I was never sure how this unwritten rule spread or why but it secured the place of the bathroom stall as a stronghold for privacy in an otherwise public corporate environment.

As I washed my hands, I counted several weeks since I had hung up the phone with P.S. 66. My company had closed for the holidays/Y2K scare and I was left with plenty of free time to debate the daunting task of contacting each and every elementary school in Saugerties, New York. The idea seemed futile and ridiculous.

As I squeezed the institutional soap into my palm, I tossed around the idea of a private detective. Something I was sure I could not afford. I immediately let that idea go the way of the soap. I took a sheet of paper towel and pondered.

Nothing seemed right. Everything seemed overkill of the inevitable: he's probably still there. He's probably still in Saugerties. I had that gut feeling. It was such a sensation that I woke up sick the next day and decided to stay home.

Around 11am, with no soap opera yet on the radar screen, I found myself caught up in another frightening and mind-numbing episode of *Jerry Springer* [I said shut up], I saw the ad again:

1-800-SEARCH-IN-USA
Over 10,000 Successful Searches
Find People Right Now!
Find Out About People, Property & more…
Easy, Low Cost, Fast
Search 100,000 Databases

Bad enough that this ridiculous and exploitative service was an easy out to my dilemma, the last thing I wanted after years of doing things the "hard way" was to use a service that sponsored this ridiculous talk show (that I seemed unable to stop watching). It seemed horrible, base and crass. It cheapened everything, made it easy, too easy. And I wondered why that bothered me so much.

Why did it have to be the hard way? Who really cared in the end if I did it one way or another? This People Search service kept popping up. Didn't that mean something? And it was the year 2000. Didn't modern technology rule our lives? How come I was not allowing myself to use it?

So I did.

The next day at work, I entered the site and followed the "fast, easy steps to finding a loved one."

The result:

Two entries matched your search criteria:

- *Laboure, Francis M. 226 Flatrush Avenue, Brookline, New York 19765*
- *Laboure, Francis J. 154 Sycamore Lane, Saugerties, New York 10537*

Total charge for this session: $15.00

I felt dirty and cheap as I put away my Master Card and clicked on the print icon. I closed the Internet connection and pondered what my next possible step could be. I had no idea.

<u>Canceling Philadelphia</u>

My search for Francis began to remind me of meeting a shady, but cute guy who gives you his number. The questions begin: should I call? Should I not call? Do I wait? Well, in this case, I had waited about nineteen years so I thought it was safe to make contact, but I still hesitated. I hadn't been having much luck with guys recently [read: at all] so I was reluctant. I was quite sure that my bad luck would overlap from my love life into my creative one. My last "real" date involved me taking a slapstick fall right in front of the gigantic window of the restaurant we were dining at. That moment had been more than enough embarrassment for one season and I was reluctant to take another "fall," this one being so much more significant.

So I waited. I went to happy hours and a few poetry readings. I dabbled with my writing, but my book was a stalemate. I thought a trip back to Philadelphia might actually help clear my head. I seemed to do well when I traveled. But, in the end, I had to cancel. I just didn't feel enough pull to bring me back and it was a city that had been my worst time creatively as long as I could remember, the exception being my current dry spell right in my home state of New York. My excuse to not visit was the housewarming party most of my friends were attending.

And so it happened that I met someone. And I liked him. A lot.

Love was as simple as that.

I had been in love before and it had been complicated and heart wrenching. It was the wrong time and long distance and too soon and too hard. It was yearning and longing and tragic. It was fodder for epic, sad poems. It was creative matter for essays and rants. I was never happy and somehow that seemed "right." Too much *Days of Our Lives* had clouded my sensibilities. For me, a relationship with or without love was always the same except for one thing: love complicated things more. Attachment made it harder to let go. Love was almost never worth it.

But things happen that way for a reason, I suppose. You meet people who are the most annoying, uninteresting individuals in existence so that when you come across the one who's not, he'll stand out. And there he was. Taking me to dance when no music was playing. Chauffeuring me to a movie in a gigantic old station wagon. Sitting in an empty theater telling me he had rented it out just for me. Telling me that the roof was leaking when I saw a tear in his eye. I hadn't expected him. He surprised me. And he kept surprising me all the time.

I had stumbled onto something completely different than what I had been looking for. Someone who looked at me and saw a girl and a woman, an angel and a devil, a writer and a typist, a butterfly and a worm, and didn't choose which one he wanted, but loved them all. After years of catering to and nursing the wounds of my lovers, for once I felt I was the one unworthy of what I had been given. The feeling was overwhelming and I was sure that it was not meant for me. His name said it all: Thomas. I immediately doubted. I wrote out of pain. I wrote out of longing and heartache. Simply put: this would never do.

<u>Awaiting the Fall</u>

It was Spring and I was torn. Some days I was a stagnant puddle of putrid water. A waste of space. I did nothing with my book. I hated myself. I came to work everyday and faced the mundane, relentless task of typing appraisals but told everyone I was writing a book. I was a liar. I started to write a book and I stopped. I could not face that printed page – "Search Results." I could not stand the idea of going to Francis. I could not call him. I could not face him. I would rather have died.

Then other days I was brilliantly happy. I watched the world outside changing, I watched the birds dance, bugs crawl. I typed appraisals. I wrote poems. I continued to fall more in love with Tom. In fact, I fell so hard it shook me to the very core of my being. I could put my pen to paper, open my mouth and I'd find butterflies, flowers and puppies darting forth. Only beautiful things, beautiful images. I was basking in it, dancing in it. I swam in it, bathed in it. And, the more I did, the less inclined I was to face Francis.

I mean, who needed him? Look at all I had. It was springtime and my love life was good for the first time in a long time. I was waking up in the morning anxious to greet the day. I was feeling wonderful about my personal life. I could deal with the drudgery of my professional life. I had met my match.

But, then, I would see that page, remember the book, get asked the question "How's your book coming?" and for a brief second, I was again a stagnant puddle of nothingness. A dark hole. A failure.

This was my torment: as long as the search continued, I would continue to feel discontent, but I feared finding Francis. I was confident in my new relationship with Tom but there was this immense unknown lingering, this gigantic "what if?" I had found love with Tom. What if my cosmic search for Francis revealed something, what if the search led to a connection? Why would I want to ruin what Tom and I had by seeking out this stranger?

I wanted to blame love for making me give up the search. Yet, surprisingly, it was our relationship that prevented me from giving up finding Francis altogether. I had once thought that love was the person who would tell me to forget it all, forget my life, leave it all behind and come follow him. That love was the blinding force that would make me forget about my pen and spend my time only with my lover. But I was wrong. That's not love. Love is the one who kisses you, holds you, strokes your hair and then with a deep voice, looks you in the eyes and asks, "So, how is your book coming? Did you write today?"

Tom was my conscience. He told me that the search was important and that I might never be truly satisfied until it was over. The search was an integral part of my success, my fulfillment and, even more, my happiness. And I did want this happiness to endure.

But, facing all of this, I still could not write. I could not face Francis. I was caught up in the emotions of loyalty and fidelity. Why did searching for Francis feel disloyal? I had to get these melodramatic visions from my mind and continue forward. I had to take that chance.

I allowed the summer of 2000 to slowly drift by and I continued to be creative in finding ways to not write: work is busy, I need to make time for the gym, my boss won't let me change my hours to give me time to write.

Francis slept in a locked drawer. I spent those months talking about him, thinking about him but never going to him. I skipped a writer's conference to go to a luau. I spent the day cleaning out my basement instead of writing my book. I secretly imagined the scenario of a fire breaking out and my manuscript burning into ashes, lost forever. I had my back to Francis and there was no sign of me turning around anytime soon.

But eventually, things changed. The summer's end brought a new boss and a new work schedule. The days got colder and, as I went into hibernation, my book slowly came out of it. I did the simplest thing I could think of: I read it again. By doing so, I saw my writing as a fulfillment to a promise I had made to myself long before babies were born, work was begun and love walked in. I was ready to take up the

reigns again and renew the search. The air was becoming chilled with

autumn and I vowed to find Francis before the last leaf fell off the tree.

IV. The End Again

Cristina T. Lopez

Killing Grandma

My resignation at the end of the summer was strong and sincere. But, as usual, life events shaped my path as much as my will.

Labor Day weekend, the summer's end, the beginning of my new work schedule, the anticipated breaking point of my seemingly endless writer's block, and the time my grandmother fell ill. A recurring infection took a bad turn and I spent lengthy periods of time in the hospital at my grandmother's, and mother's, sides.

I realized early on that I was there more for my mother than my grandmother. The longer my grandmother stayed in the hospital, the more I realized how intolerable she was. Abuela's incessant discussion about death had been heightened by her hospitalization: God had now decided not to kill her. Instead, he had given her something small and painful only to make her suffer, but not strong enough to kill her off. Her litany about death was constant, her bitterness brutal. She verbally abused my mother and took potshots at every doctor and nurse who didn't shower her with attention. Nothing was good enough in the "prison" she was trapped in. Needless to say, we were the ones who felt like prisoners.

Her constant litany was: "Never get this old. Die young." I would try to explain that if her wish had come true, I'd never been born. She scoffed. That was logic and there is no room for logic in self-pity. Her constant scowl itself was pitiable, but I could not muster the sympathy she was looking for as I sat in the private wing of St. Luke's Roosevelt Hospital overlooking the Hudson River with my mother, father, brothers, room service, concierge and private nurse. She believed this was hell, this was suffering. I knew better. But her words of advice did have an effect on me: they made me grateful that my mother was not like her and made me want to never be like her.

The constant discourse on dying, her ever-steady pronouncements on what we should do when she dies, and her post-mortem "game plan" (to bathe in the fires of hell, then go to read the riot act to St. Peter for not killing her off sooner blah, blah, blah) only made me laugh. She made me think of death as the last act to the play. There was still the encore, but the live show was over. Her constant reminder about death made it seem everyday, made it seem normal, as part of life. Maybe not the best one, but a part all the same.

In the hospital, I was with her in a moment of real suffering as they changed the bandage on her wound. I held her hand. For the tenth time that day she told me never to live to her age (89). I thought to myself that with all the talk about life being too short for most, it isn't for everyone. For some, it's painfully long. I looked at my grandmother and finally felt the pity that I could not muster before, but not for the reasons she wanted me to. I pitied her because she felt the way she did. I was sorry that I could not change her mind. Was she too old? I was not sure. What I was sure about was that she was like this at 89, but she was also like this at 79 and 69 and probably 59, too. As long as my brothers or I could remember, she had been this way. She had always wanted to die. And she would continue to be this way, until the day she really did die. And then wouldn't it be too late to take it all back?

Despite this obsession with dying, I believed my grandmother would, at the moment of death, regret wasting so much time wishing for it. Even if for just a split second, she would. She would feel it. I was sure of it. I could tell sometimes in her faraway look when she thought no one was watching. It was there: the desire to *not* die, the desire to stay alive. It was there when she took her pills like clockwork every day, three times a day. It was there when she refused to ever leave the house…except to see her doctor at least every month. It was there when she actually laughed. It was in her pleasure, in her moments of weakness before a box of bonbons. Those times, though too few and far between to ever be incorporated into her nature to ever last or make a difference, were still there, sometimes.

I dreamt once I had killed my grandmother. It was an accident in my dream, but I had still done it. Strange and unnatural as it was, there was relief in that dream. But, despite what she said, what I thought or dreamt, I could never kill Abuela. I don't just mean in the obvious literal sense. I mean, I knew she could never be silenced. Her voice lived within me. It was the voice that said death was inevitable, that death was coming. It was the lesson repeated always, "No regrets, no regrets, no regrets." It reminded me that life was too short to waste on waiting to die, to not follow the path or turn every stone. Life was too short to not live up to my potential, to not be a writer, to not write my book.

Small Miracles

After several glasses of wine at my company's summer barbecue at Tavern on the Green, I told the head of the human resources department that I did not e-mail all the time, just about 95 percent of the time. He was amused at my joke, but I wasn't joking. It was totally true. E-mail had become the perfect social, creative and philosophical outlet for a writer because it is a format that feels most comfortable: writing. E-mail is like a network of pen pals that comes with immediate satisfaction, no waiting for a letter in the mail. This was instant reply. Even auto-reply was an option. As a bored typist, e-mail was a convenient and welcome diversion.

As a "searcher," the Internet had already proven useful once. I hated being reduced to "click and point" methods to find Francis because it impersonalized such a personal quest. Yet, didn't I correspond intimately with my boyfriend and best friend on-line? Didn't I reveal my secrets, make plans for the weekends, have fights, make up, exchange a recipe, and debate politics all via e-mail? What would be so wrong in maybe shooting Francis an e-mail to see if he responded? Just as a test. Just a quick hello. Just to see how I felt about talking to him. My heart raced just thinking about it. I had to go outside.

It was a Thursday in September. There was nothing particularly special about that day, nothing particularly bad. I had a cold. The sun was shining. My grandmother was still in the hospital. I discovered a nook on 49th Street with a waterfall and fountain. I was writing everyday. I only needed to draft that e-mail, make that contact. But I could not do it. I had no idea what I was going to say. I wanted to keep it short. I wanted to identify myself and see if he responded. I had no idea what I wanted to happen next. So I stayed outside.

I sipped my pretentious grandé skim latte and decided that while the fountain and waterfall were beautiful on this sunny day, the sunshine was not able to penetrate between the buildings and warm the spot where I was sitting. I was feeling cold. This place was a perfect escape, but I was finding fault with it. Was I being too picky? Maybe it was a sign not to be sitting outside but at my computer starting a search for Francis's e-mail address.

I sat unable to move. A candy wrapper floated in the fountain. Then I looked up and noticed the security cameras all around me, acting as watchful eyes upon me. This wasn't a quiet, secluded spot as I had believed. The perfect balance of the moment was about to be undone when a bird landed at my feet, chirping. It wasn't a pigeon but a robin, a small miracle in New York City.

He pecked at the ground and looked in my direction. I waited for him to move. He looked like he was waiting for me. We both did not move. I watched him do nothing. He watched me. Then he seemed to bore with me. His head jerked left, then right. He took two steps and, suddenly, he was gone. It seemed the bird was tired of waiting for me to make my move. So was I.

Matching the Search Criteria

It's hard to remember a time when e-mail wasn't part of my life. It exploded in college when I was on UNIX and has spread like wildfire ever since. Strange to think there is a whole new generation growing up right now who will never know what it is like to not have Internet access. Just like it is strange to know there are people like my parents who may never have e-mail access. Did Francis fall into that category? It appeared so.

Perhaps it was a sign that I could only take modern technology so far, but I ended my search for Francis' e-mail address empty-handed. There was no e-mail address for a Francis Laboure living in Saugerties. Despite the number of people I knew who were "connected," I had no idea what situation he was in, and his could have been one where e-mail had no significance.

So, it was back to square one. I did still think that the idea of writing to him was the safest one I could come up with. So I decided to draft a letter instead. Pen to paper. Ink to surface. Write. Write. Write.

25 September 2000

Francis J. Laboure
154 Sycamore Lane
Saugerties, New York 10537

Dear Francis,

My name is Cristina Lopez (my friends call me Tina) and I attended All Saints Elementary School in Auburndale, New York from 1979-1984 (Kindergarten through Fourth Grade). I then transferred to a nearby elementary school, St. Anthony Padua in Bayside and lost touch with almost all of my peers from All Saints School.

If you are the Francis Laboure who attended Kindergarten and First Grade with me at All Saints, I would very much like to speak to you via telephone or in person. It would mean a lot to me for reasons I would rather not get into in a letter.

Please contact me at your earliest convenience. I can be reached Monday through Friday, 10 to 6 at the number enclosed. I also can be contacted anytime via e-mail. If you are not the Francis Laboure who attended All Saints during that period of time, please contact me either way so that I know that the letter was received.

I hope that you are the person I am looking for and that you are doing well almost twenty years later!

Sincerely,

Cristina T. Lopez

Post-Mail Trauma

I mailed the letter.

That night I dreamt they found a tumor on my spine.

I was paralyzed.

I could not write.

<u>Execution</u>

The truth is…I'm worried my book sucks. I had this great idea for a book and I told all my friends about it and they loved it. I talked about it at parties and people said it sounded great. My parents never got tired of telling their friends that their daughter was writing a novel, even though it wasn't a novel. I felt like everything in my life – my slacker job, my laziness, and my lack of career motivation – were all explained away by the idea that I was writing a book.

But, deep down, my fear is that I explain my book, my idea, and my story a lot better than I write it. I'm terrified that the idea is good but the execution is a failure. I'm wondering if maybe I am not a writer after all, that maybe I have no business working on a book or that anyone can subscribe to *Writer's Digest*, but not everyone truly has talent.

Then there is the other component: the irony of selling myself as a writer, a poet, a storyteller, to anyone who will listen but, when I finally muster the nerve to write a letter to the person I have been looking for and writing about all this time, the subject of my book, the reason why I

decided to try and become an author never was mentioned. I acted like

that part of me, the writer, did not exist. It was as if I wanted to remain

pure to him, not lie to him like I lie to everyone else. So, I left it out of

my letter.

I felt at that moment of contact that my book was something dirty,

something to hide, even though I've bragged about it for two years. I

was afraid of what he'd think if he knew. Then I was afraid of what

everyone else would think if they knew I thought that. Then I thought,

"What writer thinks this much about what other people think?"

And then I got angry. Then I was frustrated. I felt cornered and

beaten but strong. And then I wrote. I threw down a thick and burly

poem, so powerfully, so willfully, that it almost tore the paper. It read

back so robust that it left a taste in my mouth – a mixture of ink and

lead and mulch and acid. And I read it over and over and it was so much

a part of me, it made me cry. It felt right. It felt good. It felt like an

extension of my soul. I held it and it almost burned my fingertips, burning with so much life. So I dropped it and I let it cool while I stared at it. But, as I walked away, the feeling went away. So, my soul remains tortured.

Where does it all fit in? Where do I fit in? Who am I? Am I a liar for calling myself a writer or a liar for denying it? I feel that the answer is obtainable. It's in the writing of every poem, it is in the scripted letters of this book and it's at the bottom of every page. It's in the combination of words and sentences and paragraphs and the stories they become. It's strong and sure and confident. It's positive and special. It's more than one search. It's more than one book, one poem. It's every time I write. It's there, I just need to grasp it and not let it go.

The search was about finding the confidence to write and discovering the words hidden beneath the edge of my pen. If Francis never responded, if he never surfaced, I would still have my words. That's all I needed. That's all I wanted. So that's what I did: I continued to write.

<u>Contact</u>

Two days later, my phone rang. The 914 area code on my caller I.D. clued me in to the possibility that it was one of the many bed-and-breakfasts I had called that morning looking for vacancies for the peak fall foliage weekend upstate I was planning with Tom. We were both so excited for the trip but having difficulty finding a place to stay that late in the season.

I answered my phone as I always did: "Tina Lopez speaking."

"Hi. I'm, um, I received a letter from you," a lispy voice stammered out of the receiver. I didn't recall writing to any of the B&B's. Then I had another thought just as he said:

"I'm Francis Laboure."

"Oh…OH! Hi! Wow. I'm so glad you called." And awkwardly, the exchange began. Francis did not remember me. That immediately set the tone for the rest of the conversation.

He didn't really understand why I remembered him. I told him that I remembered most of my classmates pretty well and that he had stuck out in my mind because I had attended his birthday party and then soon after that he was gone from school.

Francis told me he didn't really remember that birthday or the party. He said his birthday isn't in June, as I had recalled, but in May. All he said about it was that it probably rained. When he said rain, I shivered.

Suddenly, my "distinctly clear" memories seemed vague and fuzzy. Did I remember how things happened accurately? I was no longer sure. But if he didn't recall the specific events, I didn't want to bring up what I remembered for fear of hurting his feelings. All the protective instincts I felt for Francis from the start came rushing out.

I tried to envision what he looked like as he spoke to me. It was during the day, so I imagined him at home. Working from home? He said he designed websites so that was possible. While I found the idea of his being creative and self-employed admirable, I wasn't truly inspired by his career choice. It seemed like lately everyone was designing websites or working with the Internet. I got this underlying impression of the homebound computer geek calling himself a website designer when all he did was play video games all day.

The cruelty of the thought shocked me back into attention. Francis was asking me about where I lived and with whom. After my parade of unspoken criticisms, I found my own answers laughable as I recounted my moving back home from Philadelphia to be a writer. Now who sounded pathetic?

Instead of revealing all, I stretched the truth by saying I had reached a nostalgic point in my life and was looking for people I once knew and then writing about the experience. He asked how my search for others was going, but I quickly changed the subject.

We caught up on our lives. His film and web-oriented projects: he had been an extra in the movie *Contact*, but the footage where he appeared was cut from the final edit. I wanted to talk to him about the film and get his impressions on its meaning, how it addressed the meaning of the universe and the after-life, but we could barely talk about the weather. I let the discussion move on to other topics.

I mentioned that I was working at the auction house. He told me he had just recently visited our website and was considering applying for a position since he was gearing to move to New York City. I was struck by the thought of one-day coming to work and running into Francis in the company canteen. Then I wondered if perhaps he was lying, saying that to force a connection that was so clearly lacking in our conversation. I was not sure of anything. I was merely searching for the next thing to say.

We chatted some more about unimportant things, slowly moving away from why I had called and inevitably toward experiences he had missed in the years after he left All Saints. He listened as I quickly described the trials and tribulations of the nuns, the priests, the rectory and the abortion clinic. He was quiet on the other end. Was he fascinated or just bored? I was getting nervous so I just kept talking. I went on about where I had been since all of that. I told Francis about the people I had kept in touch with through high school and whom I see now and again around Queens. Finally, I slowed down as I realized he didn't have much to contribute.

It was like revisiting a moment in time: Francis was shy, quiet and sweet. I was reaching out to him and I felt like the only one. His loneliness seemed to penetrate the phone line. But, again, I ended our contact without really making a difference, just like I had left his party without really reaching out to him.

The sad truth about my contact with Francis Laboure was that I had two chances in my life to make an impact on him, but, in the end, I had made none. I was not sure how to feel about that revelation. I was not sure how to go on.

<u>Rain</u>

The first person I called after speaking to Francis was Tom. I dropped the words into the receiver like a confession that I had been unfaithful.

"I got a call from Francis Laboure."

"Who?"

"Francis Laboure."

"Oh. OH! So…what did he say?"

"Not what I expected."

There were several aspects of my talk with Francis that lingered within me after our phone call. It was a mixture of relief and the emptiness that comes with relief. The hollowness that comes after you've sighed the big sigh and realize it's all over. The satisfaction of reaching your goal and the dissatisfaction of it not being at all what you expected.

I turned over the possibility that the awkwardness of our conversation stemmed from nervousness but I knew that wasn't true. I had reached this person who had been far away for so long and had nothing to say to him. No matter how long we stayed on the phone or however many follow up phone calls occurred, I don't think that feeling of disconnection would have changed.

There was a chasm between Francis and I that I had created by fabricating our encounter. There was an artificiality about the experience that I sensed and perhaps he did as well. The whole time we were speaking there were things that I knew about him, things that I suspected of him that I never said and could never say. Despite talk-show fantasies, I would never "reveal all" to Francis knowing it could hurt him. Whether or not my memories were accurate, the idea of a stranger inferring things about his life or his family could have hurt him and I had not the heart to do that.

I finally understood a truth that had not been clear during the entire process: I could never be close to Francis because I had taken Francis apart and put him back together again without him ever suspecting it. I could never be honest with him and without honesty, there could never be a connection between us. That was something I had not seen before, only after it was all said and done could I understand how far away Francis and I really were.

Aside from the realization about the inevitable distance that would always remain between Francis and myself, another detail about our talk was very striking. I could not escape the strong undertones of individual human perspective, how memories could be so tailored, so specific. Those who attend the same event can experience it so very differently. Every moment has an endless variety of perspectives, an endless array of stories emerging. This book was only one of them. It was only my story. My phone call with Francis showed me how little our stories had in common.

The melodrama of my mind wanted to believe Francis Laboure left All Saints School amidst turmoil and controversy, a precedent to the events and scandal that would unfold at All Saints years later. I wanted him to have left in a cloud of mystery that surrounded the non-attendance at his birthday party. Instead, I found out his parents didn't like the way the faculty treated the students. They thought the nuns were too gruff, too stern. They decided to try public school.

The story was almost too easy, too boring, too common. Even the larger looming mystery of why I was the only guest at his birthday party seemed mundane: it rained. When I asked about the party, he didn't seem startled into a bad memory nor did he attempt to skirt he issue. He merely said: "It always rains on my birthday." Did he say that on purpose? Did he know what I was getting at with my question?

Rain. Rain. Rain. It made sense. I recall my own memory: "An outdoor obstacle course of games such as pin-the-tail–on-the-donkey." But, I never remember playing the games. Was it raining? Did it make sense that people would be less inclined to attend an outdoor party on a rainy day? Did my mom drop me off to play in order to get me out of her hair for a few hours, not out of any type of loyalty or politeness?

It began to dawn on me that perhaps it was the weather that ruined the day, not hatred or meanness. And, perhaps, my attendance lacked any more significance than something to do on a rainy day. It was cheaper than a movie and out of the house.

And, perhaps, my cosmic tie to Francis, who barely even remembered me, whom I never even thought about until my senior year of college, was completely fabricated. Like a book, like a story by a writer who lacks one.

So, I had to ask myself the question: would this book still be written if Francis never called me back, if he never surfaced again?

I searched for that answer and could find none other.

Yes.

After my conversation with Tom, I hung up the phone and opened my e-mail. I found the most recent job postings from the human resources department and forwarded them on to the e-mail address Francis had given me. After all that, he had been connected. I clicked send and felt a strong sense of relief as I went on with my day.

Who Is Francis Laboure?

That e-mail message was the last contact I had with Francis Laboure. I never heard from him again. Not even to thank me for the job posting. Sometimes I felt as if I had never spoken to him at all, as if maybe I imagined our conversation. I could not help doubting the memories of such a significant event that had fallen so flatly on my psyche. What I had built up to be a heated moment in my life had turned into a tiny spark that was a mere twinkle on the long road ahead of me.

I clearly remember a talk I had with a friend right before graduating college. I was telling her the story of Francis Laboure. It was a simple, straightforward tale about a couple of kids, a birthday party and a short list of attendees but after a few plastic cups filled with Milwaukee's Best Brew, or "The Beast," I had spun the story into a potential made-for-TV-movie. After a few beers, I was a storytelling genius, or, perhaps, more aptly, after a few bong hits, the listener obtained much deeper meaning from the tale. Either way, her immediate reaction was that this was a love story: a story about finding my soul mate, my better half.

She was right. I have struggled with that notion every day from the moment I put my pen into my black and white marble composition notebook and began this book. In times of happiness, I have completely refuted it. In times of loneliness, I have embraced it. "Maybe there is hope for me. Maybe I will find the one."

After all the fantasies of love and romance, Francis was just another boy in my life that crossed my path. Perhaps his memory touched me at a time where I felt lost and uncertain about my life, but there was nothing more to him than what I had put upon him myself. I made Francis into more than what he should have been. He was not my prince charming or white knight. He was a guy whom I had known once and found again. That doesn't guarantee sparks. It's just a way to stem off the loneliness.

But, while *Finding Francis* was partly spawned out of loneliness, loneliness isn't always about being alone. It's about feeling alone. It's about being isolated from the world and people around you. Loneliness is the isolation I felt when I left academic institutions after eighteen years and lacked direction or focus, but felt like everyone else had them. Lacked romantic love and security, but believed that everyone else enjoyed it. Lacked true satisfaction and thought everyone else felt it. Looked at everyone else as a measurement for what I should be, how I should be, when the measurement should be born within.

I needed Francis to do that soul-searching. I needed Francis to help me look inside and see what it was that I really wanted, instead of outside myself in jobs and ex-boyfriends. Every guy I dated was like a Francis. I kept looking for the ideals I felt he embodied in the brief time I knew him: the humility, the sweetness, and the vulnerability. But it always failed because those characteristics don't translate to love. Sympathy, curiosity, maybe, but not love. Francis was not the love of my life. He never could be. So, in turn, neither could any of those guys.

I know what you want to read here and I wish I could write it for you. But I can't. I did not fall in love with Francis Laboure. I did not search the world over to come face to face with him in the pouring rain only to discover that he had been looking for me too. (See the Lifetime Network every Saturday around 2:30PM for that novel.) I fell in love with someone else. That someone is not the embodiment of Francis Laboure. That person led me to face Francis, he forced me to deal with the consequences of my search and he made me look at what I found, accept it and write about it. But, he is not Francis.

Finding Francis was my therapy, my direction, my focus, my security and my romance. It was through him that I faced up to loneliness. It was through the search or Francis that I overcame change: moves to New York, Philadelphia, and New York again. Changing jobs, changing boyfriends, changing lives. I had a place where it all belonged: a small black and white composition notebook where I wrote it all down, collected it, digested it and learned to accept it.

Francis gave me perspective. Every experience was an offering to him. His search was hope for me. Hope that out there, I might find a lost little boy, lost like me, but now all grown up. I was hoping to discover the person of humility, innocence and sweetness, a person who needs me. Francis was an inspiration to be a better person, to take care of others by taking care of myself first.

In dating, my weakness was always men with flaws. I found it endearing – the cheapness, ugliness, addictions, issues; I saw their flaws as humbling, their attempts to overcome them sweet, their lack of attention to them evidence of innocence. And, they needed me.

But, in romance as in friendship, these qualities can only be stomached for short periods of time. Then they become tiresome because, beneath it all, they lacked strength, and often dignity. Eventually, I always came back to that. I needed that. The victim has to recover, the persecuted has to overcome, or they'll remain that way forever. In attempts to find the innocents, I ran into the dependents whose void was hard to climb out of. But I always did and I kept searching.

The morning after Francis called me, I was left feeling unsure, as if all the emotions about destiny and fate I had anticipated were already present. I envisioned the great unveiling of a persona that embodied innocence and sweetness all wrapped up in maturity and strength. But the person on the phone, who seemed soft and sweet and special, didn't have that. The feelings were there lingering, but they didn't reside in the voice on the other end of the line. There wasn't an explosion of fulfillment and understanding, there was no shared brilliance. It was quiet and still and then it was over and I was left with the strangest feeling that this meeting had already occurred.

I don't mean that I had found Francis prior to that meeting. He had never called me or wrote to me or e-mailed me before that day. But I already knew him. I already knew about him. I had already found him embodied somewhere else.

Francis was fear, innocence, sweetness, shyness, and humility but there was more. There was strength to stand up after being knocked down, the ability to get up and fly away and still be a butterfly no matter how downtrodden. The power to overcome loneliness and fear. The ability to accept your mistakes and fix them. I just hadn't noticed that it was all there, that there was no "other" that could be to me what I wanted Francis to be. That Francis could never be to me what I wanted him to be. All the lost little boys had grown up. I could not spend my life taking care of them. My own happiness lay within. Looking inside and finding my true self was the only way to break the cycle of loneliness, the only way to find love.

Finding Francis is my book. The search made me look inside and find the creator hidden beneath. It made me reach out to the writer, the poet, the typist, and the voice inside and tell my story. It forced me to explore my passion. It took time but I finally emerged as what I had always suspected I could be: an author. I could no longer be afraid of what that title meant.

By the time I made contact with Francis, this book was already written. Its pages were laid out and the words inked to them. His voice, his reality, added a small part to something that had already been created, in my heart, in my mind and with my pen. The essence of the book was the mystery of him, the loss of him, the finding of him. The book was everything about him I had attributed to him. But I had created my own idea of Francis Laboure as much as I had created this book. The search was about him without ever being about him. The book is my experience of standing in the shadow of Francis' life and describing the view.

This is what I saw. This is what I learned. This is how it felt.

And now, the story is told. The book is complete. But there will always be more searches.

I keep writing.

I am a butterfly.

I fly away.

About the Author

Cristina is currently working on her second book of letters to a lost friend. In addition, she writes short fiction, personal essays and poetry.

Excerpts of *Finding Francis* have appeared in *The Griffin* and will be in *The Full Circle Journal of Poetry and Prose* in August 2003.

Cristina is a member of the International Women Writers' Guild (IWWG), a participant in the Southwest Women Poetry Exchange and was a resident poet at the Vermont Studio Center for November 2001. She's a huge fan of *Little House on the Prairie* and her husband with whom she is currently serving as a Peace Corps volunteer in Ukraine.

www.ingramcontent.com/pod-product-compliance
Lightning Source LLC
Chambersburg PA
CBHW022247290526
45785CB00015B/387